Ready® Common Core

Mathematics Instruction 5

Curriculum Associates

Project Manager: Paul Meyers
Revising Editor: Lynn Tauro
Cover Designer and Illustrator: Julia Bourque
Book Design: Scott Hoffman

ISBN 978-0-7609-8640-0
©2014—Curriculum Associates, LLC
North Billerica, MA 01862

15 14 13 12 11 10 9 8 7 6 5 4

Table of Contents

Table of Contents

Unit 1
Number and Operations in Base Ten

Knowing how to add, subtract, multiply, and divide whole numbers is important. But, you know that very few things in your life are about whole numbers. You want to download 6 new songs that are $1.49 each. You just read that the beach you love to visit is wearing away at a rate of 17.2 centimeters each year. You have 11.5 meters of fabric and will be making 5 equal-sized table covers for the science fair.

In this unit, you will multiply and divide with whole numbers. You will also learn how to work with the decimals in your life. You will compare them, add them, subtract them, multiply them, divide them, and love them!

✓ Self Check

Before starting this unit, check off the skills you know below. As you complete each lesson, see how many more you can check off!

I can:	Before this unit	After this unit
read and write decimals, for example: $80.63 = 8 \times 10 + 6 \times \frac{1}{10} + 3 \times \frac{1}{100}$	☐	☐
compare decimals, for example: $3.47 > 3.096$	☐	☐
round decimals, for example: 6.274 rounded to the nearest tenth is 6.3	☐	☐
multiply whole numbers, for example: $410 \times 16 = 6,560$	☐	☐
divide whole numbers, for example: $2,812 \div 38 = 74$	☐	☐
add and subtract decimals, for example: $20.08 + 5.15 = 25.23$	☐	☐
multiply decimals, for example: $7.25 \times 9.4 = 68.15$	☐	☐
divide decimals, for example: $18.72 \div 3.6 = 5.2$	☐	☐

Lesson 1   Part 1: Introduction
Understand Place Value

How is 10 related to place value?

We use a number system called **base ten**. This means that place value in any number is based on a pattern of tens.

Look at the following place-value models for whole numbers through thousands.

Thousands	Hundreds	Tens	Ones
1 thousand is 10 times 1 hundred	1 hundred is 10 times 1 ten	1 ten is 10 times 1 one	1 one

1,000   +   100   +   10   +   1   =   1,111

Think   Place value in decimals is just like place value in whole numbers.

Look at the following place-value models for decimal numbers through thousandths.

> **Below the table, circle all of the numbers in the equation.**

Ones	Tenths	Hundredths
1 whole is 10 times 1 tenth	1 tenth is 10 times 1 hundredth	1 hundredth

1   +   0.1   +   0.01   =   1.11

In a decimal number, a digit in one place has ten times the value of what it would have in the place to its right.

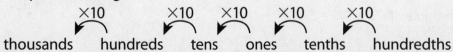

$\times 10 \qquad \times 10 \quad \times 10 \quad \times 10 \quad \times 10$

thousands   hundreds   tens   ones   tenths   hundredths

🔍 **Think** 1 hundredth is 10 times 1 thousandth.

If you break one hundredth into 10 equal parts, each of those parts is worth 1 thousandth of the whole.

Look at the pattern in the chart.

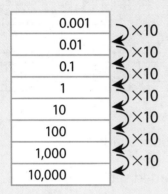

0.001
0.01
0.1
1
10
100
1,000
10,000

×10
×10
×10
×10
×10
×10
×10

When you multiply a number by 10, the product is 10 times the number.

Each time the digit 1 moves one place to the left, it is worth ten times as much. Each time the digit 1 moves one place to the right, it is worth only one tenth as much. How do you write the number that is one tenth of 0.01?

One hundredth is 10 times one thousandth.
$0.01 = 10 \times 0.001$

One thousandth is one tenth of one hundredth.
$0.001 = 0.01 \div 10$

To write the fraction one thousandth as a decimal, write a 1 in the third place after the decimal point.

$$\frac{1}{1,000} = 0.001$$

✏️ **Reflect**

1 In which number does the digit 5 have a greater value, 0.05 or 0.005? How many times as great is it, and how do you know?

_____

_____

_____

🔍 Explore It

Let's explore place-value patterns with another example using models. Each grid represents 1 whole.

A   B   C

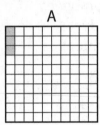 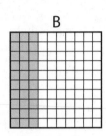 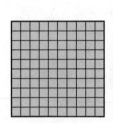 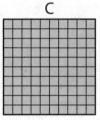 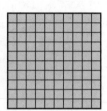

_____   _____   _____

2 Label models A, B, and C with a decimal to name the amount shaded.

3 How many times the shaded section of Model A is the shaded section of Model B?

_____

How many times the shaded section of Model B is the shaded section of Model C?

_____

4 Use the grids to complete the equations.

$0.03 \times 10 =$ _____

$0.3 \times 10 =$ _____

$0.3 \div 10 =$ _____

$3.0 \div 10 =$ _____

Now try these two problems.

5 Continue the ×10 pattern to fill in the blanks.

0.003   0.03   0.3   _____   _____   300

6 Use the ÷10 pattern to fill in the blanks.

500   _____   5   0.5   0.05   _____

Talk About It

Now let's explore how 0.30 compares to 0.3.

7 Look at the grids in problems 2 and 3. Models A and B show 3 hundredths and 3 tenths. Shade some or all of these grids to show 30 hundredths.

  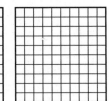

What did you label the grid from the previous page that shows the same amount?

_____

8 Use your grids to write a decimal for 30 hundredths.

thirty hundredths = _____

9 How does this show that 30 hundredths is the same as 3 tenths?

_____

_____

10 What equation can you write to represent *10 times 3 hundredths is 30 hundredths*?

_____

Try It Another Way

11 Imagine a grid shaded to show 0.001. How much would be shaded?

_____

_____

12 How would you shade a grid to show ten thousandths?

_____

🔍 Connect It

Talk through these problems as a class, then write your answers below.

13 Create: Draw a picture to show how the value of 0.04 is related to the value of 0.4. Then write a division sentence to represent your drawing.

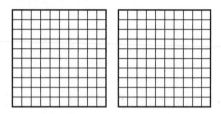

---

14 Analyze: Kiran modeled 0.08 with the diagram below.

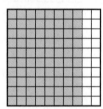

What is wrong with Kiran's model? What can be done to her diagram to show 0.08?

_____

_____

15 Demonstrate: A meter is one thousandth of a kilometer. Write an equation to show the relationship between 962 meters and 0.962 kilometers.

_____

Put It Together

16 Use what you have learned to complete this task.

A blade of grass is 0.002 meters wide, an ant is 0.02 meters long, and a brick is 0.2 meters long.

A   Use a place-value chart to show the value of each measurement.

Object	Tens	Ones	.	Tenths	Hundredths	Thousandths

B   Draw a diagram to compare the width of one blade of grass to the length of the ant.

Draw another diagram to compare the length of the ant to the length of the brick.

C   Use your diagrams to explain how many blades of grass would equal the length of one brick. Then write an equation using the measurements to show your answer.

_____

_____

_____

Lesson 2   Part 1: Introduction 👥

Understand Powers of Ten

What does it mean to multiply by 10, 100, or 1,000?

Numbers like 10, 100, or 1,000 that can be written as products of tens are sometimes called **powers of ten**. Multiplying and dividing by powers of ten is related to place value.

Look at the numbers 30, 300, and 3,000 in the place value-chart. How many tens are in the number 30?

1,000s	100s	10s	1s	
			3	
		3	0	30 = 3 × 10
	3	0	0	300 = 3 × 100 or 3 × 10 × 10
3	0	0	0	3,000 = 3 × 1,000 or 3 × 10 × 10 × 10

When you multiply 3 × 10, you really just mean 3 tens, or 30. In the same way, 3 × 100 really just means 3 hundreds or 300. Another way to write this is 3 × 10 × 10. You can think of 3 × 10 × 10 × 10 as 3 × 1,000, or 3 thousands.

🔍 **Think**   Patterns can help you understand multiplying by powers of ten.

Look at the multiplication equations that use powers of ten in the chart above. You may be able to see a pattern when you compare the number of 0s in the factors to the number of 0s in the product. In this lesson, you will explore why that pattern makes sense and how it can help you multiply and divide with powers of 10.

🔍 **Think** Dividing by 10 "undoes" multiplying by 10.

If you multiply a number by 10 and then divide it by 10, you end up with the number you started with. For example, $3 \times 10 = 30$, and $30 \div 10 = 3$. This means that division is the **inverse** of multiplication.

Dividing by 100 is the inverse of multiplying by 100. Since 3×100 is 300, you know that $300 \div 100$ means $3 \times 100 \div 100$, or 3.

How many 0s would be in the product of $3 \times 10,000$?

1,000s	100s	10s	ones	
3	0	0	0	
	3	0	0	$3,000 \div 10 = 300$
		3	0	$3,000 \div 100 = 30$
			3	$3,000 \div 1,000 = 3$

The patterns you can find in dividing by powers of ten are similar to the patterns in multiplying. Pay attention to the number of 0s in the two numbers being divided (dividend and divisor) and the number of 0s in the quotient.

In the next few pages you'll have a chance to discuss what you see.

✏️ **Reflect**

1 How many 0s are in the product of 4×100? $4 \times 1,000$? $4 \times 10,000$? How do you know?

_____

_____

_____

🔍 Explore It

Now explore patterns in decimal point placement when multiplying or dividing a decimal by a power of ten.

2 Compare the numbers 5.0 and 0.5. How many times 0.5 is 5? Use place value to explain how you know.

_____

_____

3 Compare the numbers 0.5 and 0.05. How many times 0.05 is 0.5? Use place value to explain how you know.

_____

_____

4 Now use place-value reasoning to fill in the blanks in the table below. Look for useful patterns as you work.

Ones	.	Tenths	Hundredths	Thousandths	
0	.	0	0	5	
	.				0.005 × 10
	.				0.005 × 10 × 10
	.				0.005 × 10 × 10 × 10

Remember that division is the inverse of multiplication. Use understanding of division and place value to fill in the blanks in the table below. Look for useful patterns as you work.

Ones	.	Tenths	Hundredths	Thousandths	
7	.	0	0		
	.				7 ÷ 10
	.				7 ÷ 100
	.				7 ÷ 1,000

Talk About It

Find out what happens when a decimal is multiplied or divided by a power of ten.

5 How many places does the decimal point move when you multiply a number by 10? In which direction?

_____

6 How many places does the decimal point move when you divide a number by 10? In which direction?

_____

7 What pattern describes how the decimal point moves when you multiply a decimal number by any power of ten?

_____

8 What pattern describes how the decimal point moves when you divide a decimal number by any power of ten?

_____

Try It Another Way

A shorthand for writing powers of ten can make it easier to use the patterns for multiplying and dividing. In the shorthand column, the small, raised number is called the **exponent**.

Standard Form	Product of Tens	Shorthand	Read As
10	10	10^1	10 to the first power
100	10×10	10^2	10 to the second power
1,000	$10 \times 10 \times 10$	10^3	10 to the third power

9 What is 3×10^2? _____ What is 3×10^3? _____

10 What is 0.005×10^2? _____ What is 0.05×10^2? _____

🔍 Connect It

Talk through these problems as a class, then write your answers below.

11 **Compare:** Use this place-value chart to describe the relationship between $0.8 \div 10^2$ and 0.8×10^2.

Tens	Ones	.	Tenths	Hundredths	Thousandths	
8	0	.	0	0	0	0.8×10^2
	8	.	0	0	0	0.8×10^1
	0	.	8	0	0	0.8
	0	.	0	8	0	$0.8 \div 10^1$
	0	.	0	0	8	$0.8 \div 10^2$

_____

_____

12 **Inspect:** Marisa said that multiplying 8.0 by 1,000,000 would increase the value of the 8 because there would be 6 more zeros after the decimal point. Explain what is wrong in Marisa's statement.

_____

_____

_____

_____

_____

13 **Illustrate:** Show how $7{,}000 \div 1{,}000$ is the same as $7{,}000 \div 10 \div 10 \div 10$.

_____

_____

Put It Together

14 Use what you have learned to complete this task.

> Jaime claims that when you multiply a whole number by 100, the decimal point moves 2 places to the right. Salome argues that the decimal point only moves when you multiply a decimal number by 100. When you multiply a whole number by 100, the product has 2 extra 0s.

A Explain both students' point of view, with examples.

_____

_____

_____

_____

_____

_____

_____

_____

_____

B Which student is correct? Justify your answer.

_____

_____

Lesson 3   Part 1: Introduction 👥

Read and Write Decimals

You already know how to read and write whole numbers and fractions. Reading and writing decimals is similar to both.

Jessica is reading aloud from a science website. There are various measurements in the article she is reading, such as 0.33 meter and 0.555 meter. How should she read 0.33?

🔍 Explore It

Use the math you already know to solve the problem.

Jessica can read 0.33 as 3 tenths and 3 hundredths, but it is easier to understand her if she simply says how many hundredths that is.

To read 0.33 as some number of hundredths:

◾ Write 3 tenths as a fraction. _____

◾ Rewrite 3 tenths as an equivalent fraction with a denominator of 100. _____

◾ Write 3 hundredths as a fraction. _____

◾ Complete the equation to add the like fractions for 3 tenths and 3 hundredths.

$$\frac{\boxed{}}{100} + \frac{\boxed{}}{100} = \underline{}$$

◾ Write in words how Jessica should read the number 0.33. _____

◾ Explain how you can use place value and fractions to help you know how to read a number with 2 digits after the decimal point.

_____

_____

_____

🔍 Find Out More

Sometimes, decimals are read just as strings of digits, for example: *zero point three three*. But to give meaning to the amount a decimal represents, you name the place value of the smallest-sized unit, and read the number to say how many of those units you have.

Ones	.	Tenths	Hundredths	Thousandths
0	.	3	3	

33 hundredths

The least place value in 0.33 is hundredths, so you read the decimal by saying how many hundredths it represents.

Now look at the same decimal with a zero in the thousandths place.

Ones	.	Tenths	Hundredths	Thousandths
0	.	3	3	0

330 thousandths

In the decimal 0.330, the least place value is thousandths. Even though 0.330 is exactly equal to 0.33, we read 0.330 to tell how many thousandths it represents.

The table below shows the decimal 0.555.

Ones	.	Tenths	Hundredths	Thousandths
0	.	5	5	5

555 thousandths

The least place value in 0.555 is thousandths. You read the decimal to tell how many thousandths it represents.

When a decimal number includes a whole number, read it the way you read mixed numbers. You read $3\frac{5}{10}$ as "three and five tenths." Read 3.5 as "three and five tenths."

✏️ Reflect

1 Write 1.005 as a fraction. Then write how this fraction is read aloud.

_____

_____

_____

Read the problem below. Then explore different ways to represent decimals.

Josh has been tracking the growth of his dog since it was a puppy. He uses a meter stick to measure the dog's height and records the height as 0.604 meter. Josh's mom asks, "How tall is your dog?" What does Josh tell his mother?

Model It

You can use place-value understanding to write the expanded form of 0.604.

With decimals:

$$0.604 = 0.6 + 0.004$$
$$= 6 \times 0.1 + 4 \times 0.001$$

With fractions:

$$0.604 = 6 \times \frac{1}{10} + 4 \times \frac{1}{1,000}$$
$$= \frac{6}{10} + \frac{4}{1,000}$$
$$= \frac{600}{1,000} + \frac{4}{1,000}$$
$$= \frac{604}{1,000}$$

Model It

You can write 0.604 in a place-value chart to show the place value of each digit.

Ones	.	Tenths	Hundredths	Thousandths
0	.	6	0	4

The least place value of 0.604 is thousandths.

🔍 Connect It

Now you will write the word form of the decimal on the previous page using both models.

To read a decimal, you tell how many of the smallest fractional part it represents.

2 Look at the place-value chart. What are the names of the four place values in 0.604?

_____

Which of those places has the least value? _____

3 Look at the expanded notation with fractions. How many thousandths are there in 0.604? _____

4 What is the word form of 0.604?

_____

5 What is the word form of 1.604? _____

6 Explain how reading the digits after the decimal point and knowing the name of the least place is enough information to read a decimal number. Use the examples 0.604 and 1.604 in your explanation.

_____

_____

_____

_____

✏️ Try It

Use what you just learned about identifying the least place value to read decimal numbers.

7 What is the word form of 0.44? _____

8 What is the word form of 1.057? _____

Read the problem below. Then explore different ways to think about writing the numbers as decimals.

Nobu heard a sports news report that said Abha finished a running race one and sixteen thousandths of a second ahead of Nadia. Brianne finished two and thirty-five hundredths seconds ahead of Chandra. What decimals represent these measurements?

🔍 Model It

Model the measurements with mixed numbers and expanded form.

Write mixed numbers to show the number of whole seconds and then the fraction of a second given by each measurement. Then expand.

one *and* sixteen thousandths

$$1\frac{16}{1,000}$$

$$1 + \frac{16}{1,000}$$

$$1 + \frac{10}{1,000} + \frac{6}{1,000}$$

$$1 + \frac{1}{100} + \frac{6}{1,000}$$

two *and* thirty-five hundredths

$$2\frac{35}{100}$$

$$2 + \frac{35}{100}$$

$$2 + \frac{30}{100} + \frac{5}{100}$$

$$2 + \frac{3}{10} + \frac{5}{100}$$

🔍 Model It

Ones	.	Tenths	Hundredths	Thousandths
1	.	0	1	6
2	.	3	5	

16 thousandths is
10 thousandths and 6 thousandths or
1 hundredth and 6 thousandths

35 hundredths is
30 hundredths and 5 hundredths or
3 tenths and 5 hundredths

Connect It

Now you will use the models to write the numbers on the previous page as standard decimals.

9 Compare the mixed-number and the place-value representation of *one and sixteen thousandths*. How does each model show the whole number of seconds?

_____

_____

10 How does each representation of *one and sixteen thousandths* show the value of the fractional part of a second?

_____

_____

11 How can you write *one and sixteen thousandths* as a decimal? _____

12 How does each representation of *two and thirty-five hundredths* show the value of the fractional part of a second?

_____

_____

13 How can you write *two and thirty-five hundredths* as a decimal? _____

14 Explain how you can write the standard form of a decimal given in word form.

_____

_____

_____

Try It

Use what you just learned to write these numbers as decimals.

15 six and two hundred three thousandths _____

16 ten and seventy-five hundredths _____

Study the model below. Then solve problems 17–19.

What place-value relationship lets me write $\frac{50}{1,000}$ as $\frac{5}{100}$?

> **Student Model**
>
> The height of Coach Roberts is two and fifty-four thousandths meters. Write this height with numerals.
>
> **Look at how you could show your work using expanded form.**
>
> Two and fifty-four thousandths is $2\frac{54}{1,000}$.
>
> $$\frac{54}{1,000} = \frac{50}{1,000} + \frac{4}{1,000}$$
> $$= 5 \times \frac{10}{1,000} + 4 \times \frac{1}{1,000}$$
> $$= 5 \times \frac{1}{100} + 4 \times \frac{1}{1,000}$$
> $$= 5 \times 0.01 + 4 \times 0.001$$
>
> | Ones | . | Tenths | Hundredths | Thousandths |
> |------|---|--------|------------|-------------|
> | 2 | . | 0 | 5 | 4 |
>
> Solution: **2.054 meters**

Pair/Share

Why can you use fractions to represent a decimal number?

What mixed number could represent 14.895?

17 Aubrey runs the 100 meter dash in 14.895 seconds. What words could you use to read 14.895?

Show your work.

Pair/Share

Is there a different way to use words to represent 14.895?

Solution: _____

18 Paulo measured the width of a sideline on a football field. It was one hundred two thousandths of a meter. What is this width in expanded form?

Show your work.

How is this number represented in a place-value chart?

Solution: _____

_____

19 Which of the following is a representation of 4.082? Circle the letter of the correct answer.

A $4 + \frac{8}{10} + \frac{2}{1,000}$

B four and eighty-two thousandths

C four and eight and two hundredths

D $4 + 8 \times \frac{1}{10} + 2 \times \frac{1}{100}$

Rachel chose **D** as the correct answer. How did she get that answer?

_____

_____

_____

_____

What are the place values of each digit in 4.082?

Solve the problems.

1   Daniel ran the 400 meter dash in 89.023 seconds. Which of the following expresses this time in words?

     A   eighty-nine and twenty-three hundredths seconds

     B   eighty-nine and two tenths and three thousandths seconds

     C   eighty-nine and twenty-three thousandths seconds

     D   eighty-nine thousand twenty three seconds

2   What decimal represents $6 \times 1{,}000 + 2 \times 10 + 3 \times \frac{1}{10} + 5 \times \frac{1}{1{,}000}$?

     A   6,020.305

     B   6,200.350

     C   6,020.035

     D   6,002.035

3   One guitar string that plays a very high note is eleven thousandths of an inch thick. A string on a bass that plays a very low note is ten times as thick. For each quantity, choose either *Yes* or *No* to tell whether it is equal to ten times eleven thousandths.

     a. $\frac{1}{100} + \frac{1}{1{,}000}$ ☐ Yes   ☐ No

     b. $\frac{1}{10} + \frac{1}{100}$ ☐ Yes   ☐ No

     c.   0.11   ☐ Yes   ☐ No

     d.   eleven hundredths   ☐ Yes   ☐ No

     e.   eleven ten thousandths   ☐ Yes   ☐ No

4 Which of the following correctly represent 57.036? Circle the letter for all that apply.

A $57 + \frac{3}{100} + \frac{6}{1,000}$

B $57 + 3 \times \frac{10}{1,000} + 6 \times \frac{10}{1,000}$

C $57 + 36 \times 0.01$

D $57 + 36 \times 0.001$

E fifty-seven and thirty-six hundredths

5 Represent 240.149 in two different ways. Then explain how each way shows the place value of the digits of the number.

_____

_____

_____

_____

_____

_____

_____

6 Alex wrote 103.903 in expanded form as $100 + 3 \times 1 + 9 \times \frac{1}{100} + 3 \times \frac{1}{1,000}$. Explain his mistake. Then tell how to correct it.

_____

_____

✓ **Self Check** *Go back and see what you can check off on the Self Check on page 1.*

Lesson 4   Part 1: Introduction 👥

Compare and Round Decimals

You already know how to compare and round whole numbers. In this lesson, you will use place-value understanding to compare and round decimals.

Grace is sorting buttons by size for a craft project. Blue buttons are 0.008 meter wide, and red ones are 0.02 meter wide. Which button is wider?

🔍 Explore It

You can compare these decimals by reasoning about place-value relationships.

▪ What are the place values of the 8 and the 2?

8 is in the _____ place.

2 is in the _____ place.

▪ Compare those place values: There are _____ thousandths in 1 hundredth.

▪ How do you know that 8 thousandths is less than 1 hundredth?

_____

▪ Write an inequality statement using < or > to compare 0.008 and 0.01. _____

▪ Now think about whether 0.02 is greater or less than 0.01. Write an inequality statement to compare 0.008 and 0.02. _____

▪ Explain how you know this inequality statement is correct.

_____

_____

_____

▪ Which button is wider? _____

Find Out More

To compare decimals, you may think about equivalent expressions for the same number in different ways.

Words	Place value	Fractions
10 hundredths is 1 tenth	$0.10 = 0.1$	$\frac{10}{100} = \frac{1}{10}$
10 thousandths is 1 hundredth	$0.010 = 0.01$	$\frac{10}{1,000} = \frac{1}{100}$
100 thousandths is 1 tenth	$0.100 = 0.1$	$\frac{100}{1,000} = \frac{1}{10}$

Using these equivalent expressions can help you see that, since 8 thousandths is less than 10 thousandths, $0.008 < 0.010$.

Using equivalent expressions can also help you understand how to round decimals. To round 0.008 to the nearest hundredth is to choose whether it is closest to 0.00, 0.01, 0.02, 0.03, and so on.

You round a number down when it is less than halfway between two values. When a number is more than halfway, or exactly halfway, between the two values, you always round it up.

But, what *is* halfway between 0 and 0.01, or halfway between 0.01 and 0.02?

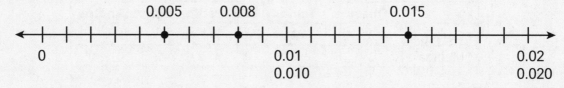

Since half of 10 thousandths is 5 thousandths, halfway from 0 to 0.010 is 0.005. Since 0.008 is more than halfway from 0 to 0.01, round it to 0.01.

Reflect

1 Is 0.013 more or less than halfway between 0.01 and 0.02. How do you know?

_____

_____

_____

Read the problem. Then explore different ways to compare decimals.

Gary's walk to school is 3.275 kilometers. Melissa's walk to school is 3.24 kilometers. Who walks farther to get to school? Who lives farther away from school?

Model It

Express the two distances as mixed numbers with like denominators.

$3.275 = 3\frac{275}{1,000}$

Gary lives $3\frac{275}{1,000}$ kilometers from school.

$3.24 = 3\frac{24}{100}$

$3\frac{24}{100} = 3\frac{240}{1,000}$

Melissa lives $3\frac{240}{1,000}$ kilometers from school.

Model It

Write the distances in a place-value chart.

	Ones	.	Tenths	Hundredths	Thousandths
Gary	3	.	2	7	5
Melissa	3	.	2	4	0

Gary lives 3,275 thousandths kilometers away from school.

Melissa lives 324 hundredths kilometers away from school.

Melissa lives 3,240 thousandths kilometers away from school.

Connect It

Now you will use the two models on the previous page to explore the same problem.

The fraction model shows $3\frac{24}{100}$ as $3\frac{240}{1,000}$. The place-value model shows 3.24 as 3.240.

2 Both models change the way the fractional part or decimal part of 3.24 is represented. What is the same about how the denominator and the place value change? _____

3 What is the same about how the numerator of the fraction and the digits after the decimal change? _____

_____

4 How does rewriting the fractional part or decimal part of 3.24 make it easier to compare it to 3.275? _____

_____

_____

5 Explain how you can use what you know about comparing 240 and 275 to help you compare $3\frac{240}{1,000}$ with $3\frac{275}{1,000}$ or compare 3.240 with 3.275. _____

_____

_____

Try It

Use what you just learned about comparing decimals to solve these problems. Show your work on a separate sheet of paper.

6 Heather bought 5.190 ounces of frozen yogurt. Jeff bought 5.195 ounces of frozen yogurt. Write an inequality statement comparing the weights of their yogurts.

_____

7 Brayden and his cousin Kayla live twenty miles away from each other. On the same day, Brayden records 1.046 inches of rain at his house and Kayla records 1.062 inches of rain at her house. Whose house received less rain that day? _____

Read the problem. Then explore different ways to round the decimal.

Maura has a shelf that is 2.97 meters long. She is buying craft boxes that are 0.273 meter long. Maura wants to round these numbers to the nearest tenth to estimate about how many boxes will fit on the shelf.

Model It

Place 0.273 on a number line to see its relationship to nearby tenths.

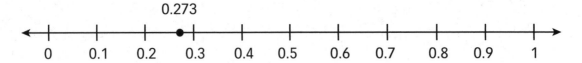

0.273 is between 0.2 and 0.3, and closer to 0.3.

Model It

Compare 2.97 to nearby tenths.

Ones	.	Tenths	Hundredths
2	.	9	
2	.	9	1
2	.	9	2
2	.	9	3
2	.	9	4
2	.	9	5
2	.	9	6
2	.	9	7
2	.	9	8
2	.	9	9
3	.	0	0

2.97 is more than halfway, and rounds up to 3.0.

Connect It

Now compare the two ways to think about rounding numbers.

8 On the number-line model, how is the halfway point between the two nearby tenths shown? _____

_____

9 In the table, how is the halfway point between the two nearby tenths shown?

_____

10 To the nearest tenth, how long is the shelf? _____

11 To the nearest tenth, how long is a craft box? _____

12 About how many boxes will fit on the shelf? How do you know?

_____

13 Explain how you can tell by looking at the digit after the place you want to round to whether the number is more or less than halfway between the nearby tenths?

_____

_____

14 Describe how each model can help you round. _____

_____

_____

15 When a number is exactly at the halfway mark, you round it up. Round 0.25 to the nearest tenth. _____

Try It

Use what you just learned about rounding decimals to solve these problems. Show your work on a separate sheet of paper.

16 A dropper holds 0.813 milliliters of fluid. What is this amount rounded to the nearest hundredth? _____

17 At the end of each month, Belinda earns $0.024 for every dollar in her savings account. Round this to the nearest hundredth to show about how many cents she earns for $1.00. _____

Study the model below. Then solve problems 18–20.

Student Model

Rounding decimals is like rounding whole numbers.

Makayla weighed 3.747 kilograms at birth. Her brother John weighed 3.477 kilograms at birth. Whose birth weight was about 4 kilograms?

Look at how you could show your work using a number line.

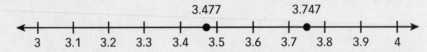

The point representing Makayla's birth weight is closer to 4 kilograms than the point representing John's birth weight.

Solution: __Makayla_____

Pair/Share

How do the birth weights compare?

How do I use place value to round whole numbers and decimals?

18 A grocery store charges customers for produce to the nearest hundredth of a pound. If Landon purchases 2.386 pounds of tomatoes, what weight did the store charge for?

Show your work.

Pair/Share

About how many pounds of tomatoes? About how many tenths of a pound?

Solution: _____

19 Ellie fills her car with 14.297 gallons of gas. Alivia fills her car with 14.209 gallons of gas. Write an inequality statement comparing the two gas purchases.

Show your work.

How do I use place value to compare numbers?

Solution: _____

20 Which of the following comparisons is NOT true? Circle the letter of the correct answer.

A $42.300 = 42.3$

B $5.020 < 5.20$

C $0.149 < 1.490$

D $108.308 > 108.4$

Ava chose **A** as the correct answer. How did she get that answer?

_____

_____

_____

_____

Am I supposed to compare the number of digits, or compare the place value of the digits?

Solve the problems.

1 The weights of four similar packs of tomatoes are listed below.

Pack A: 2.456 pounds
Pack B: 2.457 pounds
Pack C: 2.454 pounds
Pack D: 2.459 pounds

Malcolm rounds the weights to the nearest hundredth. Which pack's weight does NOT round to 2.46?

A Pack A

B Pack B

C Pack C

D Pack D

2 Which comparison is NOT true?

A $1.78 < 1.92$

B $1\frac{78}{100} < 1\frac{92}{100}$

C $1 + 7 \times \frac{1}{10} + 8 \times \frac{1}{100} < 1 + 9 \times \frac{1}{10} + 2 \times \frac{1}{100}$

D $1 + \frac{70}{10} + \frac{80}{100} < 1 + \frac{9}{10} + \frac{2}{100}$

3 Tori and Alvin use a stopwatch to record the amount of time it takes a marble to roll down a four-story ramp. Tori's marble takes 2.845 seconds, while Alvin's marble takes 2.835 seconds. Tell whether each sentence is *True* or *False*.

a. Rounded to the nearest tenth, both times are the same. ☐ True ☐ False

b. Rounded to the nearest hundredth, both times are the same. ☐ True ☐ False

c. Both times are closer to 2.8 than 2.9. ☐ True ☐ False

d. Both times are more than halfway between 2.84 and 2.85. ☐ True ☐ False

e. Alvin's marble was faster. ☐ True ☐ False

4 Lauren is going to have soup for dinner, but she doesn't want more than 0.92 grams of sodium. Decide if each brand of soup has less than, greater than, or exactly 0.92 grams of sodium. Write each brand in the correct category in the chart.

Brand A: 0.920 g   Brand B: 0.875 g   Brand C: 0.915 g   Brand D: 1.100 g

Less than 0.92 grams	Equal to 0.92 grams	Greater than 0.92 grams

5 The weights of four packages of meat are shown below.

Package A	1.748 lb
Package B	1.645 lb
Package C	1.754 lb
Package D	1.532 lb

Part A

Each package is priced by how much it weighs to the nearest tenth of a pound. Order the packages from greatest to least price.

Show your work.

Answer _____

Part B

Explain how the order would change if you rounded the weights to the nearest hundredth.

_____

_____

_____

✓ **Self Check** *Go back and see what you can check off on the Self Check on page 1.*

Lesson 5   Part 1: Introduction 👥

Multiply Whole Numbers

In grade 4, you multiplied two-digit numbers by two-digit numbers. Now you'll multiply three-digit numbers by two-digit numbers. Take a look at this problem.

A school is designing a new backstage for the auditorium. The available space for the project is 173 feet by 36 feet, with plans for the prop area to have a width of 30 feet, and the dressing room area to have a width of 6 feet. What is the area of the available space in square feet?

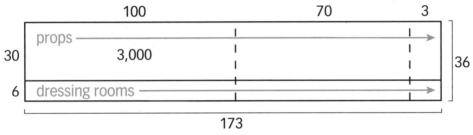

🔍 Explore It

Use the math you already know to solve the problem.

The area model above shows the width of each room.

▪ What is the total length of the model? _____ What is the total width? _____

▪ How is each partial product found? _____

_____

▪ How can you find the total area? _____

▪ The product of 173 and 36 is the total area of the backstage space. How can you find the area for props? _____

How can you find the area for the dressing room? _____

_____

▪ What is the total area? _____

Find Out More

To multiply, you can use place value to break apart one or both factors into a sum of other numbers, and then multiply each of those numbers by the other factor. Add the **partial products** to find the product.

$$173 \times 36 = 173 \times (30 + 6)$$

3 tens and 6 ones

First, find each partial product.

$$
\begin{array}{r}
173 \\
\times\ 30 \\
\hline
5{,}190 \\
\end{array}
\qquad
\begin{array}{r}
173 \\
\times\ 6 \\
\hline
1{,}038 \\
\end{array}
$$

partial products

Then find the sum of the two partial products because you need to combine the products of the factor you broke apart.

$$
\begin{array}{r}
173 \\
\times\ 36 \\
\hline
1{,}038 \\
+\ 5{,}190 \\
\hline
6{,}228 \\
\end{array}
$$

← area for dressing room
← area for props
← total area backstage

Reflect

1 How is multiplying by a 2-digit number the same as multiplying by a 3-digit number?

_____

_____

_____

Read the problem below. Then explore different ways to multiply a three-digit number by a two-digit number.

There are 128 cups in a full package. How many cups are in 35 full packages?

Model It

Use an area model to multiply a three-digit number by a two-digit number.

128 × 35

128 is 1 hundred, 2 tens, and 8 ones, or 100 + 20 + 8.

35 is 3 tens and 5 ones, or 30 + 5.

	100	20	8
30	30 × 100 = 3,000	30 × 20 = 600	30 × 8 = 240
5	5 × 100 = 500	5 × 20 = 100	5 × 8 = 40

First row: 3,000 + 600 + 240 = 3,840

Second row: 500 + 100 + 40 = 640

So, 128 × 35 = 3,840 + 640 = 4,480.

Model It

Use the distributive property to find partial products and add them.

128 × 35 = 128 (30 + 5)

128(30 + 5) = (128 × 30) + (128 × 5)

$$\begin{array}{r} 128 \\ \times\ \ 30 \\ \hline 240 \\ 600 \\ +\ 3,000 \\ \hline 3,840 \end{array}$$
240 (30 × 8)
600 (30 × 20)
+ 3,000 (30 × 100)

> 30 × 8 = 10 × 3 × 8
> 30 × 20 = 10 × 3 × 20
> 30 × 100 = 10 × 3 × 100

$$\begin{array}{r} 128 \\ \times\ \ \ 5 \\ \hline 40 \\ 100 \\ +\ 500 \\ \hline 640 \end{array}$$
40 (5 × 8)
100 (5 × 20)
+ 500 (5 × 100)

3,840 + 640 = 4,480

Connect It

Now you will solve the problem from the previous page using partial products.

2 Why is the area model divided into six sections? _____

_____

_____

3 How do the three steps in each partial-products equation relate to the three sections in each row of the area model? _____

_____

4 Would the product change if 30 and 5 on the left side of the area model were changed to 20, 10, and 5? Explain. _____

_____

_____

_____

5 List two different ways you could break up the factors in 239×64 to find the product. Explain why both ways would have the same product. _____

_____

_____

_____

Try It

Use what you just learned about multiplying numbers to solve this problem. Show your work on a separate sheet of paper.

6 A bookshelf at a library holds 156 books. There are 15 bookshelves in the children's section. How many children's books can the library place on the bookshelves?

_____

Study the model below. Then solve problems 7–9.

Student Model

Why does the product of 366 and 2 tens have a 0 in the ones place?

There are 366 days in a leap year and 24 hours in a day. How many hours are in a leap year?

Look at how you could show your work using the standard algorithm.

$$\begin{array}{r} \overset{1\ 1}{\underset{2\ 2}{}} \\ 366 \\ \times\ \ 24 \\ \hline 1{,}464 \\ +\ 7{,}320 \\ \hline 8{,}784 \end{array}$$

Solution: 8,784 hours

Pair/Share

What was done with a regrouped amount when finding the product of two digits?

What is the role of place value when multiplying two numbers?

7 A dishwasher uses about 29 kilowatts per hour. If a dishwasher is used 156 hours in a year, how many kilowatts of energy were used that year?

Show your work.

Pair/Share

Show and explain how to solve this problem using a different method.

Solution: _____

8 If a stamp costs 45 cents, what does a roll of 125 stamps cost in cents? What is this amount in dollars?

Show your work.

How could I first estimate the answer to this problem?

Solution: _____

🗨 **Pair/Share**

Why is multiplication used to solve this problem? What other operation is used?

9 Raquel can type an average of 63 words per minute. Rick can type an average of 73 words per minute. How many more words can Rick type than Raquel in 135 minutes? Circle the letter of the correct answer.

A 1,350

B 4,599

C 8,505

D 9,855

Jared chose **B** as the correct answer. How did he get that answer?

_____

_____

_____

_____

How can I use partial products to find the number of words typed?

🗨 **Pair/Share**

Does Jared's answer make sense?

Solve the problems.

1 Mrs. Cady constructs a cube with 512 magnetic blocks. Students in her two classes will each make an identical cube. There are 28 students in one class and 25 students in the other class. How many blocks does she need for all her students?

A 5,120

B 12,800

C 14,336

D 27,136

2 What are the values of the regrouped amounts?

$$
\begin{array}{r}
\overset{2\,3}{435} \\
\times\ \ 17 \\
\hline
3{,}015 \\
+\ 4{,}350 \\
\hline
7{,}365
\end{array}
$$

A 2 and 3

B 20 and 3

C 200 and 30

D 2,000 and 300

3 Choose either *Yes* or *No* to tell whether the expression is equivalent to 179×44.

a. 179(4 + 4) ☐ Yes ☐ No

b. (179 × 40) + (179 × 4) ☐ Yes ☐ No

c. (100 × 4) + (70 × 4) + (9 × 4) ☐ Yes ☐ No

d. 4,000 + 2,800 + 360 + 400 + 280 + 36 ☐ Yes ☐ No

e. (100 × 44) + (70 × 44) + (9 × 44) ☐ Yes ☐ No

4   Show two different ways to complete the multiplication problem.

$$
\begin{array}{r}
3\ 1\ 4 \\
\times \quad\quad 5\ \square \\
\hline
1\ \square\ \square\ \square\ 6
\end{array}
\qquad
\begin{array}{r}
3\ 1\ 4 \\
\times \quad\quad 5\ \square \\
\hline
1\ \square\ \square\ \square\ 6
\end{array}
$$

5   Barry stacks 78 boxes of DVDs in a warehouse. Each box has 116 DVDs. Nineteen of the boxes are shipped. How many DVDs are left in the warehouse?

Show your work.

Answer _____ DVDs

6   Use the distributive property two different ways to find the product of 127 and 32.

Show your work.

✓ **Self Check**   *Go back and see what you can check off on the Self Check on page 1.*

Lesson 6   Part 1: Introduction 👥

Divide Whole Numbers

In the last lesson, you learned how to find products of two- and three-digit factors. Now you will learn how to divide with two-digit divisors.

There are 345 fifth graders enrolled at Wilson Middle School and 15 fifth-grade classrooms. How many students are in each class if each class has the same number of students?

🔍 Explore It

Use the math you already know to solve the problem.

- What multiplication equation can you use to solve $345 \div 15$? _____

- Multiply 15 by multiples of 10. Fill in the blanks.

    $15 \times 10 =$ 150 $15 \times 20 =$ 300 $15 \times 30 =$ 450

- Now estimate the quotient. The quotient will be between which two tens? _____

- If $15 \times 20 = 300$, what number is left after you subtract this product from 345? _____

- Divide what is left by 15.   45 $\div\ 15 =$ 3

- Explain how to use the information above to find $345 \div 15$.

    _____

    _____

    _____

Find Out More

On the previous page, you used the relationship between multiplication and division along with properties of operations to divide.

This thinking can also be shown using an area model. It is similar to an area model used for multiplication. With division, the product is known, and you need to find a missing factor.

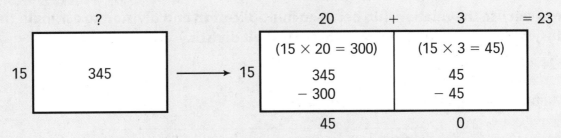

Start with the greatest place and find the quotient place by place. On the previous page, you estimated the quotient to be between 20 and 30. So, 20 is the greatest ten that can be in the quotient.

- Start by multiplying 15×20.

- Subtract the product from 345.

- Write the difference, 45, in the next section of the model.

- Think $15 \times ? = 45$. Multiply 15 by 3 and subtract this product from 45.

- The difference is 0, so there is nothing left to divide.

Reflect

1 How is the dividing with an area model similar to multiplying with an area model? How is it different?

_____

_____

_____

_____

Read the problem below. Then explore different ways to divide by a 2-digit divisor.

A grocery store only sells eggs by the dozen. If there are 624 eggs in stock, how many dozens of eggs are there?

🔍 Model It

You can use the relationship between multiplication and division to estimate the answer to a division problem with a two-digit divisor.

$624 \div 12 = ?$ and $12 \times ? = 624$

Multiply 12 by multiples of 10. Make a table.

dozens	10	20	30	40	50	60
eggs	120	240	360	480	600	720

The quotient is between 50 and 60.

🔍 Model It

You can use an area model to solve a division problem with a two-digit divisor.

```
        ?
  ┌──────────────┐
12│     624      │
  └──────────────┘
```

→

```
        50        +        2      = 52
  ┌──────────────┬──────────────┐
  │(12 × 50 = 600)│(12 × 2 = 24) │
12│    624       │     24       │
  │  − 600       │   − 24       │
  └──────────────┴──────────────┘
       24              0
```

Connect It

Now you will record the calculations from the model as partial quotients.

2 How many hundreds are in the dividend? _____
How many groups of 12 are in 600? _____
This partial quotient is written above the bar.

How is this shown in the area model?

_____

```
  52 ← quotient
   2 ← partial quotient
  50 ← partial quotient
12)624
 − 600
   24
 − 24
    0
```

3 Why is 600 subtracted from 624?

_____

4 How does the area model relate to finding the second partial product?

_____

_____

5 Show how to use the partial quotients to find 624 ÷ 12. _____

_____

6 Describe how to divide using partial quotients. _____

_____

_____

_____

_____

Try It

Use what you just learned about dividing by a 2-digit divisor to solve these problems. Show your work on a separate sheet of paper.

7 An elementary school has a total of 1,134 seeds to plant. The seeds will be placed in 27 rows. How many seeds can be planted in each row? _____

8 Nathan writes an essay with a total of 583 words. There is an average of 11 words per line. How many lines long is Nathan's essay? _____

Study the model below. Then solve problems 9–11.

Student Model

Why is 80 a good number to use first?

Each package has 21 pieces of chalk. How many packages can be made with 1,701 pieces of chalk?

Look at how you could show your work using partial quotients.

$$\begin{array}{r} 81 \\ \hline 1 \\ 80 \\ 21\overline{)1{,}701} \\ -\,1{,}680 \leftarrow 21 \times 80 \\ \hline 21 \\ -\,21 \leftarrow 1 \times 21 \\ \hline 0 \end{array}$$

Solution: __81 packages__

Pair/Share

How can you use multiplication to check the quotient?

You can first estimate how many glasses of each size can be filled.

9 A water cooler holds 1,284 ounces of water. How many more 6-ounce glasses than 12-ounce glasses can be filled from a full cooler?

Show your work.

Pair/Share

Explain how you found your estimate.

Solution: _____

10 Each student gets 35 craft sticks to make an art project. The art teacher has 7,140 craft sticks. There are enough craft sticks for how many students?

Show your work.

What friendly numbers can I use to estimate?

Solution: _____

 Pair/Share
Explain how to check the answer to a division problem.

11 Harrison creates balloon animals for different events. He has 6,440 balloons. He wants to use the same number of balloons for each of 28 events. How many balloons can Harrison use at each event? Circle the letter of the correct answer.

A 23

B 203

C 230

D 2,030

What will be the greatest place in the quotient?

Tina chose **A** as the correct answer. How did she get that answer?

_____

_____

_____

Pair/Share
Does Tina's answer make sense?

Solve the problems.

1 Which equation can NOT be represented by the model below?

```
         ?
   ┌──────────────────┐
42 │      5,964       │
   └──────────────────┘
```

A 5,964 − ? = 42

B 5,964 ÷ ? = 42

C 42 × ? = 5,964

D 5,964 ÷ 42 = ?

2 Vera makes a table to help solve the problem 672 ÷ 16. Which is the best estimate of the quotient?

10	20	30	40	50	60
160	320	480	640	800	960

A a number between 30 and 40

B a number close to 40

C about 52

D a number between 50 and 60

3 Use the grid to draw a rectangle with an area of 1,125 square units and a side of 25 units.

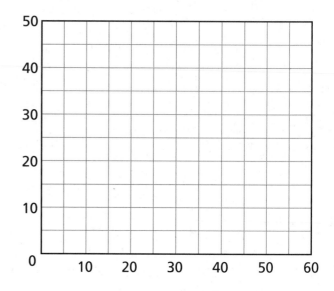

4 Lisa's camera has 2,048 megabytes of memory for storing pictures. She has already used half this amount. A high-quality picture uses 16 megabytes of memory. How many high-quality pictures can Lisa store with the remaining memory?

_____

5   Mr. Kovich writes the problem $32 \times \triangle = 1{,}696$ on the board. Write a division equation that can be used to find the value of the triangle, and then find the value of the triangle.

Show your work.

Answer _____

6   Mr. Sullivan is organizing teams for the middle school's annual field day. There are eight classes at the school and 21 students in each class.

Part A

What is the total number of students at the school?

Answer _____

Part B

Mr. Sullivan wants to have 12 students on each team. How many teams will there be?

Answer _____

Part C

How many fewer students will be on each team if he decides to have 24 teams? Explain your answer using diagrams, pictures, mathematical expressions, and/or words.

Answer _____

 **Self Check**   *Go back and see what you can check off on the Self Check on page 1.*

Lesson 7   Part 1: Introduction

Add and Subtract Decimals

In grade 4, you learned to add whole numbers by combining the values of digits in the same position. Now you'll add decimals the same way. Take a look at this problem.

Sabrina and Christie run in a relay. Sabrina runs 100 meters in 13.25 seconds, and Christie then runs the same distance in 12.2 seconds. What is their total time?

Explore It

Use the math you already know to solve the problem.

▪ About how many seconds did the girls run altogether? _____ Explain your reasoning.

_____

_____

▪ You can think of Sabrina's time as 1 ten + 3 ones + 2 tenths + 5 hundredths. Write Christie's time in the same way. _____

▪ Combine Sabrina's and Christie's times. How many tens in all? _____ How many ones in all? _____ How many tenths in all? _____ How many hundredths in all? ____

▪ Write the decimal that names the sum. _____

▪ How does the sum compare to your estimate? Is your answer reasonable?

_____

▪ Use words to explain how you could find Sabrina and Christie's total time.

_____

_____

Find Out More

You can use what you know about adding whole numbers to add decimals. To add 13.25 and 12.2, you combine like place values.

One way to add decimals is to write the numbers vertically. Lining up the decimal points is a way to keep track of like place values. Using a place-value chart can help.

Tens	Ones	.	Tenths	Hundredths
1	3	.	2	5
1	2	.	2	0

$\frac{2}{10}$ is equivalent to $\frac{20}{100}$, so you can write a 0 in the hundredths column.

Sum: 2 tens + 5 ones + 4 tenths + 5 hundredths = 25.45

The total time is 25.45 seconds.

If you want to find the difference between Sabrina's and Christie's times, subtract 12.20 from 13.25. The same rules that you use for subtracting whole numbers apply to subtracting decimals.

Tens	Ones	.	Tenths	Hundredths
1	3	.	2	5
1	2	.	2	0

$\frac{2}{10}$ is equivalent to $\frac{20}{100}$, so you can write a 0 in the hundredths column.

Difference: 0 tens + 1 one + 0 tenths + 5 hundredths = 1.05

Christie ran faster by 1.05 seconds.

Reflect

1 How could you find the sum of 9.3 and 7.55? Explain how you know your answer makes sense. _____

_____

_____

_____

_____

Read the problem below. Then explore different ways to understand how to add decimals to solve the problem.

From his apartment, Tim rides the bus 3.82 miles. Then he walks 0.4 mile from the bus stop to school. How many miles does Tim travel from home to school?

Picture It

You can picture adding two decimals on a number line.

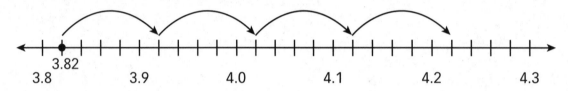

Starting at 3.82, you can make 4 jumps of 0.1 of a mile to the right to show the sum of 3.82 and 0.4.

Model It

You can use a place-value chart to help you understand how to add decimals.

	Ones	.	Tenths	Hundredths
Home to stop	0	.	4	0
Stop to school	3	.	8	2

The sum is 3 ones + 12 tenths + 2 hundredths.

💡 Connect It

Now you will use the picture and the model to help you understand how to add decimals.

2 How can you use the number line in Picture It to figure out how many miles Tim travels from home to school? _____

_____

_____

3 Look at Model It on the previous page. What is another way to express 12 tenths?

_____

What is another way to express the sum? _____

4 You can add the decimals without a place-value chart by writing them vertically, lining up the decimal points to keep track of place values.

$$\begin{array}{r} 3.82 \\ + \ 0.40 \\ \hline \end{array}$$

Why do you align the 8 in 3.82 with the 4 in 0.40? _____

5 The addition problem to the right is partially completed. Explain why there is a 1 above the ones place.

$$\begin{array}{r} \overset{1}{3.82} \\ + \ 0.40 \\ \hline .22 \end{array}$$

_____

_____

6 Complete the problem. How many miles does Tim travel from home to school?

_____

7 Explain how to add decimals.

_____

✏️ Try It

Use what you just learned about adding decimals to solve this problem. Show your work on a separate sheet of paper.

8 Yana makes a trail mix with 128.25 grams of dried fruit and 41.8 grams of almonds. How many grams of trail mix did Yana make? _____

Read the problem below. Then explore different ways to subtract decimals.

Marty cuts 2.05 ounces of cheese from a 4.6 ounce block of cheddar. How many ounces of cheddar are left in the block?

🔍 Picture It

You can subtract decimals using base-ten models.

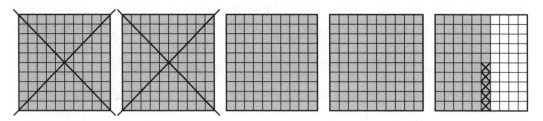

Model 4 wholes and 6 tenths.

6 tenths = 60 hundredths

🔍 Model It

You can subtract decimals using a place-value chart.

Using a place-value chart helps you make sure the place values are lined up the right way.

	Ones	.	Tenths	Hundredths
Original amount	4	.	6	0
Amount cut	2	.	0	5

Connect It

Now you will use the picture and the model to understand how to subtract decimals.

9 Look at the base-ten model on the previous page. Explain why parts of the model are crossed out. _____

_____

10 According to the picture, how many ounces of cheddar are left in the block? _____

_____

11 Look at the place-value chart in Model It on the previous page. Why can't you just subtract the 5 from the 6? _____

_____

_____

12 You can subtract the decimals without a place-value chart by writing them vertically, lining up the decimal points to keep track of place values.

$$\begin{array}{r} 4.60 \\ -\,2.05 \\ \hline \end{array}$$

13 Another way to express 6 tenths is _____ tenths + 10 hundredths. So you can rewrite the problem as

$$\begin{array}{r} {}^{5\ 10} \\ 4.\cancel{6}0 \\ -\,2.05 \\ \hline \end{array}$$

Complete the subtraction problem. There are _____ ounces of cheddar left.

14 Explain how to subtract two decimals and how to tell if your answer is reasonable.

_____

_____

_____

Try It

Use what you just learned about subtracting decimals to solve this problem. Show your work on a separate sheet of paper.

15 Gwen is sending a box to a friend. The box weighs 23.5 pounds. Gwen removes a 4.47 pound book to decrease the shipping cost. What is the new weight of the box?

_____

Study the model below. Then solve problems 16–18.

The student needed two steps to solve the problem.

Student Model

Diana has 3 different beads on her necklace. The red bead is 0.68 centimeter long. The multi-colored bead is 1.22 centimeters long, and the blue bead is 0.8 centimeter long. What is the total length of the beads on Diana's necklace?

Look at how you could show your work using equations.

$$
\begin{array}{r}
\overset{1}{1.22} \\
+\ 0.68 \\
\hline
1.90
\end{array}
\qquad
\begin{array}{r}
\overset{1}{1.90} \\
+\ 0.80 \\
\hline
2.70
\end{array}
$$

$$0.68 + 1.22 + 0.8 = 2.7$$

Solution: **2.7 centimeters**

Pair/Share

Does it matter in what order you add the decimals?

How many hundredths are equivalent to 7 tenths?

16 Outdoor cats have an average lifespan of 3.18 years. Indoor cats have an average lifespan of 16.7 years. About how much longer do indoor cats live than outdoor cats?

Show your work.

Pair/Share

How do you know what operation to use to solve this problem?

Solution: _____

17 Kenton is shopping for clothes at a twelfth anniversary sale. He buys a pair of jeans priced at $24.99 and a clearance-priced shirt for $5.25. The store discounts his entire purchase by $12.12. How much does Kenton pay for his clothes?

Show your work.

This problem takes more than one step to solve.

Solution: _____

⌨ **Pair/Share**

Explain how to check if your answer was reasonable.

18 Three boxes of cereal weigh 379.4 grams, 424.25 grams, and 379.37 grams. What is the difference between the lightest and heaviest box?

A 44.15 grams

B 44.85 grams

C 44.88 grams

D 45.12 grams

Cambria chose **D** as the correct answer. How did she get that answer?

What operation will solve this problem?

_____

_____

_____

⌨ **Pair/Share**

How could Cambria have checked her answer?

Solve the problems.

1 Randy rode his bike 1.23 miles to school from his house. After school, he rode 0.9 mile farther to the library. Randy biked home along the same route, stopping at a park 1.05 miles from the library. How many miles is the park from Randy's house?

A 3.18

B 2.37

C 1.08

D 0.27

2 Tim tracked the change in outside temperature one afternoon. He recorded a temperature of 85.4°F at noon. The temperature then rose 3.85°F over the next 4 hours. At 5:00 PM, Tim recorded a temperature of 89.25°F. How did the temperature change between 4:00 PM and 5:00 PM?

A The temperature increased 0.8°F.

B The temperature decreased 0.2°F.

C The temperature increased 1°F.

D There is no change in temperature.

3 Tell whether each equation is *True* or *False*.

a. $198.5 - 42.81 = 155.69$

☐ True   ☐ False

b. $73.27 + 251.6 = 98.43$

☐ True   ☐ False

c. $37.04 + 56.20 = 93.6$

☐ True   ☐ False

d. $70.64 - (9.3 + 29.36) = 90.7$

☐ True   ☐ False

e. $38.2 - (11.11 + 23.76) = 3.33$

☐ True   ☐ False

4 The sum of three decimal numbers is 6. Exactly one of the numbers is less than 1. What could those numbers be?

Show your work.

Answer _____

5   Choose **all** the models or expressions that represent the difference, 3.7 − 1.02.

A

B

C   2 ones + 6 tenths + 8 hundredths

D

E

6   Ryan and Sarah are looking at cell phone plans. A group plan will cost an average of $120.95 per month. An individual plan will cost an average of $62.77 per month. Should Ryan and Sarah purchase a group plan or two individual plans? Justify your answer. How much money could they save?

Show your work.

_____

_____

✓ **Self Check**   *Go back and see what you can check off on the Self Check on page 1.*

You know how to multiply whole numbers by whole numbers and whole numbers by fractions. Take a look at this problem.

Margo has 6 cubes of equal size. The sides of the blocks are 0.8 inch long.

If Margo places all the blocks in a row with sides touching, how long is the row?

🔍 Explore It

Use the math you already know to solve the problem.

▪ First, estimate the side of each block to the nearest inch. _____

▪ Estimate the length of the row of 6 blocks using your answer. _____

▪ Will the actual length be more or less than your estimate? _____

▪ Why? _____

▪ The side of each block is _____ tenths of an inch. There are _____ blocks in the row.

▪ How many tenths of an inch long is the row of blocks? _____ tenths of an inch

▪ Write the decimal equivalent:

The length of the row is _____ inches.

▪ Is your answer reasonable? Explain your thinking.

_____

▪ Use your own words to explain how you could find the length of the row.

_____

_____

🔍 Find Out More

On the previous page, you saw that $6 \times 0.8 = 4.8$. How is this related to $6 \times 8 = 48$?

Notice that the digits of 6×0.8 are the same as the digits of 6×8. The digits of their products are also the same. Why is this?

In earlier lessons, you learned that dividing by 10 or multiplying by 0.1 shifts the decimal point to the left so the value of the number is less by a factor of 10.

Look at the table below to see patterns when you multiply numbers by 0.1 and 0.01.

Expression	Equivalent Expressions	Product
6×8	$6 \times 8 \times 1.0$ 48×1.0	48.0
6×0.8	$6 \times 8 \times 0.1$ 48×0.1	4.8
6×0.08	$6 \times 8 \times 0.01$ 48×0.01	0.48

Notice that the decimal point moves one place to the left each time we multiply by 0.1.

✏️ Reflect

1 What is the product of 6×0.008? Explain your reasoning.

_____

_____

_____

Read the problem below. Then explore different ways to understand multiplying by hundredths.

> Padma bought 3 pounds of grapes. Grapes cost $2.75 for each pound. How much money did Padma spend on grapes?

🔍 Picture It

You can use decimal grids to picture multiplying with hundredths.

Think of 3 × $2.75 as 3 groups of 2.75.

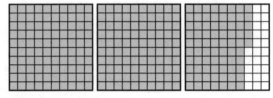

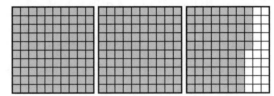

🔍 Model It

You can use partial products to multiply with hundredths.

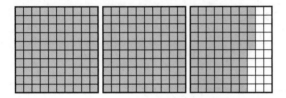

$$
\begin{array}{r}
2.75 \\
\times \quad 3 \\
\hline
\end{array}
$$

15 ⟵ 3 ones × 5 hundredths   =   15 hundredths

210 ⟵ 3 ones × 7 tenths = 21 tenths = 210 hundredths

+ 600 ⟵ 3 ones × 2 ones = 6 ones   = 600 hundredths

825 hundredths

Connect It

Use what you know about decimals and place value to solve the problem.

2 To solve the problem, you need to find 3 × $2.75. Estimate the total cost of the grapes. Explain your thinking. _____

3 Look at Picture It. How many full grids can you make? _____

How many squares would be shaded in the partially filled grid? _____

4 Look at Model It. How is multiplying with decimals like multiplying with whole numbers? _____

_____

5 Complete the following:

825 hundredths = _____ tenths

825 hundredths = _____ ones

6 Both Picture It and Model It show that 3 × $2.75 = _____

Is the product reasonable? Explain. _____

_____

7 Explain how to multiply a whole number by a decimal in the hundredths.

_____

_____

Try It

Use what you have learned about multiplying by hundredths to solve these problems. Show your work on a separate sheet of paper.

8 Bananas cost $0.65 per pound. Sasha bought 4 pounds of bananas. How much did she pay for the bananas? _____

9 Brian creates a chain of 11 paper clips. Each paper clip is 2.48 centimeters long. How long is the chain of paper clips? _____

Read the problem below. Then explore different ways to multiply tenths by tenths.

Hayden made a sign that is 1.4 meters long and 1.2 meters wide to post on the wall of his store. How many square meters of wall space will the sign cover?

 **Picture It**

You can use an area model to multiply tenths by tenths.

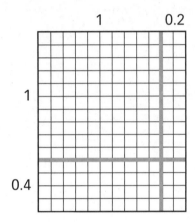

The rectangle measures 1.4 meters by 1.2 meters.

The area of each small square is 0.01 square meter.

Model It

You can use partial products to multiply tenths by tenths.

$$
\begin{array}{r}
1.2 \\
\times\ 1.4 \\
\hline
\end{array}
$$

8 ← 4 tenths × 2 tenths = 8 hundredths

40 ← 4 tenths × 1 one = 4 tenths = 40 hundredths

20 ← 1 one × 2 tenths = 2 tenths = 20 hundredths

+ 100 ← 1 one × 1 one = 2 ones = 100 hundredths

168 hundredths

Connect It

Now you will use the model and properties of operations to solve the problem.

10 To solve the problem, you need to find 1.4 × 1.2. Estimate the area of the sign. Explain your thinking.

_____

11 Look at Picture It. Complete the area model to find the area of each of the four sections of the rectangle.

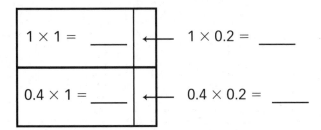

12 Look at Model It. How do the partial products relate to the area model?

_____

_____

13 Both Picture It and Model It show that 1.4 × 1.2 = _____ square meters.

Is the product reasonable? Explain. _____

_____

_____

14 Explain what you know about the product when you multiply tenths by tenths.

_____

_____

Try It

Use what you have learned about multiplying by tenths to solve these problems. Show your work on a separate sheet of paper.

15 Rosa filled her car's tank with 9.8 gallons of gas. Each gallon cost $3.85. How much did Rosa spend on gas? _____

16 Harry has 0.5 bottle of water in his game bag. Each bottle holds 0.9 liter of water. How many liters of water does Harry have? _____

Study the model below. Then solve problems 17–19.

The student wrote 1.25 as 1 + 0.2 + 0.05 and used an area model to solve the problem.

Liam ate 0.5 of a 1.25 ounce bag of raisins. How many ounces of raisins did Liam eat?

Look at how you could show your work using a model.

	1	0.2	0.05
0.5	$0.5 \times 1 = 0.5$	$0.5 \times 0.2 = 0.10$	$0.5 \times 0.05 = 0.025$

$$0.5 + 0.10 + 0.025 = 0.625$$

Solution: 0.625 ounces

Pair/Share

Solve the problem without a model.

I multiply tenths by tenths to solve this problem.

17 Gina rides her bike to work at an average of 10.4 miles per hour. She bikes 1.2 hours each day. About how many miles does Gina ride each day?

Show your work.

Pair/Share

What is a reasonable estimate for this problem? Explain your thinking.

Solution: _____

18 If a person's hair grows about 1.2 centimeters a month, about how much would it grow in 9 months?

Show your work.

Will the product be in tenths or hundredths?

Solution: _____

Pair/Share

Solve the problem using an area model.

19 Find the product of 1.05 and 0.7. Circle the letter of the correct answer.

A   73.5

B   7.35

C   0.735

D   0.0735

Aaron chose **C** as the correct answer. How did he get that answer?

_____

_____

_____

_____

Will the product be greater or less than 1.05?

Pair/Share

Does Aaron's answer make sense?

Solve the problems.

1 Which of the following has a product of 25.16?

A   3.7 × 680

B   3.7 × 68

C   3.7 × 6.8

D   3.7 × 0.68

2 Willa downloads 5 songs. Three of the song files are each 2.75 MB, and two song files are each 3.8 MB. How much space does Willa need for the songs she downloads?

A   5.55 MB

B   11.55 MB

C   15.85 MB

D   27.75 MB

3 Choose **all** the expressions that have the same value as the product of 0.11 and 4.5.

A   0.495 × 0.01

B   0.495 × 0.001

C   49.5 × 0.01

D   495 × 0.01

E   495 × 0.001

4 The area model below can be used to represent the product of 2.8 and 1.3. Complete the model by writing the following numbers in the correct positions.

| 0.6 | 2 | 0.24 | 0.8 |

	2	0.8
1		
0.3		

5 Tyrone said that 2.35 × 5 equals 1.175 because there is only one digit before the decimal point in 2.35, so there must be one digit before the decimal point in the product. Use pictures, numbers, or words to explain whether or not Tyrone is correct.

Show your work.

6 Each product below is missing a decimal point.

Part A

Place the decimal point in each example so that the equation is correct.

$$12.53 \times 5 = 6265$$

$$4.28 \times 3.6 = 15408$$

$$1.3 \times 0.89 = 1157$$

$$7 \times 6.12 = 4284$$

Part B

Circle one of the equations. Explain how you decided where to place the decimal point in this equation.

✓ **Self Check** *Go back and see what you can check off on the Self Check on page 1.*

Lesson 9   Part 1: Introduction 👥

Divide Decimals

CCSS
5.NBT.B.7

Now that you know how to multiply with decimals, you'll learn how to divide with decimals. Take a look at this problem.

> Mr. Kovich is preparing materials for a craft project. He has 2 meters of string and needs to cut it into pieces that are 0.2 meter long. How many 0.2-meter pieces can he cut from 2 meters of string?

🔍 Explore It

Use the math you already know to solve the problem.

▪ You need to find how many groups of 0.2 meter are in 2 meters. Look at the drawing below.

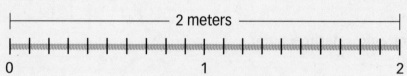

▪ How many tenths of a meter are in 1 meter? _____

In 2 meters? _____

▪ Circle groups of 2 tenths. How many groups of 2 tenths are in 1 meter? _____

In 2 meters? _____

▪ Explain how you could find how many 0.2-meter pieces can be cut from 2 meters of string.

_____

_____

_____

Find Out More

On the previous page, you saw that 2 ÷ 0.2 = 10. Notice that the digits are the same as in 2 ÷ 2 = 1.0, but the quotients differ by a factor of 10.

Look at the table below to see some patterns.

Expression	Expression in words	Quotient
2 ÷ 2	How many groups of 2 are in 2?	1
2 ÷ 0.2	How many groups of 0.2 are in 2?	10
2 ÷ 0.02	How many groups of 0.02 are in 2?	100

When the divisor is greater than 1, the quotient is less than the dividend. When the divisor is less than 1, the quotient is greater than the dividend.

Reflect

1 Look at the table above. What do you think 2 ÷ 0.002 equals? Explain your reasoning.

_____

_____

_____

_____

Read the problem below. Then explore different ways to understand dividing a decimal by a whole number.

> Coach Ann is setting up a 2.7-kilometer race. She uses flags to mark off 9 equal sections of the race. How far apart should she space the flags to mark off the sections?

 **Picture It**

You can draw a bar model to represent the problem.

You know the number of kilometers to be divided into equal groups and the number of groups.

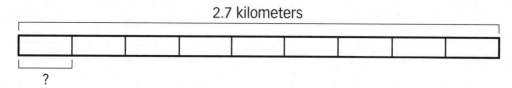

Model It

You can use the relationship between multiplication and division to understand the problem.

To find 2.7 ÷ 9, think 9 × ? = 2.7.

    2.7 = 27 tenths

    9 × ? = 27 tenths

Connect It

Now use your understanding of division and place value to solve the problem.

2 Look at Picture It. Why is the bar divided into 9 equal parts?

_____

What do you need to find? _____

3 Look at Model It. How does the division expression 2.7 ÷ 9 relate to the bar model?

_____

_____

4 Explain how you know that 2.7 = 27 tenths.

_____

5 How far apart should Coach Ann space the flags? _____ tenths of a kilometer.

Write that answer as a decimal: _____ of a kilometer

6 Explain how you could divide a decimal by a whole number.

_____

_____

Try It

Use what you have learned about dividing a decimal by a whole number to solve these problems. Show your work on a separate sheet of paper.

7 How much will each person receive if $20.35 is split equally among 5 people? _____

8 What is 0.99 ÷ 11? _____

Read the problem below. Then explore different ways to divide by tenths.

Grant has 3.6 pounds of pretzels. He puts the pretzels into bags that can each hold 0.3 pound. How many bags does Grant use to hold the pretzels?

🔍 Picture It

You can picture dividing by tenths with decimal grids.

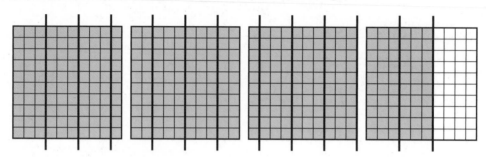

Each large square represents 1 pound of pretzels.

You know the amount to be shared equally and the size of each group.

🔍 Model It

You can use the relationship between multiplication and division to understand the problem.

To find 3.6 ÷ 0.3, think 0.3 × ? = 3.6.

   3.6 = 36 tenths

Use words to describe the problem situation:

   3 tenths × ? = 36 tenths

Connect It

Now use your understanding of division and place value to solve the problem.

9 Look at Picture It. How do you decide what to shade?

_____

_____

_____

10 Why are the columns in the grids separated into groups of 3?

_____

_____

11 Look at Model It. How do you know this is a division problem?

_____

_____

12 Explain why 3.6 = 36 tenths. _____

_____

13 Both Picture It and Model It tell me that Grant uses _____ bags of pretzels.

14 Explain how to divide tenths by tenths. _____

_____

Try It

Use what you have learned about dividing by tenths to solve these problems. Show your work on a separate sheet of paper.

15 How many dimes are there in a jar of dimes worth $2.70? _____

16 What is 42 ÷ 0.7? _____

Read the problem below. Then explore different ways to divide by hundredths.

Fiona has $1.20 with which to buy some elastic tape. The elastic tape is on sale for $0.08 per foot. How many feet of elastic tape can Fiona buy?

Picture It

You can picture the division problem using a bar model.

You know the total amount of money and the size of one group.

$1.20

?

$0.08

Model It

You can use the relationship between multiplication and division to understand the problem.

To find 1.20 ÷ 0.08, think 0.08 × ? = 1.20.

1.20 = 120 hundredths

Use words:

8 hundredths × ? = 120 hundredths

Connect It

Use your understanding of division and place value to solve the problem.

17 Look at Picture It. What are you trying to find in this problem?

_____

18 What operation will solve this problem? How do you know?

_____

_____

19 Explain why 1.20 = 120 hundredths. _____

_____

20 Write a division expression for the situation. _____

21 How many feet of elastic tape can Fiona buy? Show your work.

_____

22 Check your answer using the decimals in a multiplication equation:

_____ feet of elastic tape × $_____ = $_____

Fiona can buy _____ feet of elastic tape.

23 Explain how to divide by a decimal in the hundredths. _____

_____

_____

Try It

Use what you have learned about dividing by hundredths to solve these problems. Show your work on a separate sheet of paper.

24 How many quarters are in a jar of quarters worth $9.75? _____

25 What is 16 ÷ 0.16? _____

Study the model below. Then solve problems 26–28.

The student wrote a related multiplication equation to solve the problem.

Student Model

Nancy used 2.5 gallons of gas to drive 35 miles. How many miles per gallon did Nancy's car get?

Look at how you could show your work using equations.

$$2.5 \times \boxed{} = 35$$

$$2.5 = 25 \text{ tenths}, 35 = 350 \text{ tenths}$$

$$25 \times \boxed{} = 350$$

$$350 \div 25 = 14$$

Nancy's car got 14 miles per gallon.

Solution: 14 miles per gallon

Pair/Share

Can you solve the problem in another way?

What is a good estimate for your answer?

26 What number multiplied by 8 will give a product of 9.6? Write an equation and solve.

Show your work.

Pair/Share

How could you model this problem with a number line?

Solution: _____

27 The width of a math textbook is 0.75 inches. How many math textbooks can be placed standing up on a shelf that is 18 inches wide?

Show your work.

Will the answer be greater or less than 18?

Solution: _____

Pair/Share

Explain how you decided what operation to use to solve the problem.

28 What is 6.5 ÷ 0.5? Circle the letter of the correct answer.

A 3.25

B 6

C 7

D 13

Gwen chose **A** as the correct answer. How did she get that answer?

_____

_____

_____

_____

I could draw a model to represent this problem.

Pair/Share

Does Gwen's answer make sense?

Solve the problems.

1 Jordan has $20 to spend at the used book store. Each book costs $2.85. How many books can Jordan buy?

  A 4

  B 5

  C 6

  D 7

2 Keith bought 3.4 pounds of peanuts on Monday, 2.5 pounds on Tuesday, and 4 pounds on Wednesday. He is going to divide them equally among himself and two friends. How many pounds of peanuts will each friend get?

  A 99 pounds

  B 33 pounds

  C 9.9 pounds

  D 3.3 pounds

3 A sticker is 1.2 centimeters wide. How many stickers will fit edge to edge on a strip of paper that is 108 centimeters long?

  ☐ stickers

4 If you put 0.7 on the blank for each equation below, will it make the equation true? Select *Yes* or *No* for each equation.

  A _____ × 5.2 = 36.4 ☐ Yes ☐ No

  B 49 ÷ _____ = 70 ☐ Yes ☐ No

  C _____ ÷ 3.5 = 0.02 ☐ Yes ☐ No

  D 9.1 × _____ = 13 ☐ Yes ☐ No

5 Jamie has 5 jars to fill with beads for a carnival game. She has 7.5 cups of multi-colored beads. How many cups of beads can she place into each jar?

Part A

Use pictures to solve the problem.

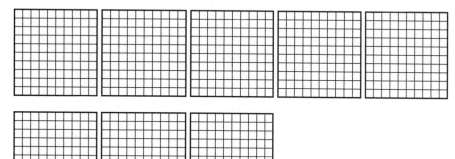

Answer _____ cups

Part B

Justify your answer.

Solve the problems.

1 Which number is equivalent to 0.15×10^3?

- **A** 0.015
- **B** 0.15
- **C** 15
- **D** 150

2 The driving distance between Buffalo, NY, and Rochester, NY, is 117.456 kilometers. What is this distance rounded to the nearest tenth?

- **A** 117 km
- **B** 117.5 km
- **C** 117.46 km
- **D** 120 km

3 Julie rides her bike a lot during summer vacation. In June, she rode her bike 104.78 miles. In July, she rode 129.53 miles. In August, she rode 61.05 miles. Which statement is true? Circle the letter for all that apply.

- **A** Julie rode more than twice as many miles in July as in August.
- **B** Julie rode a total of 295.36 miles during summer vacation.
- **C** Julie rode 43.73 miles more in June than in August.
- **D** Julie rode more miles in June than in July.

4 The table shows the lengths of the five keys that Paco has on his keychain.

Key Label	Length (inches)
T	2.104
G	1.793
W	2.079
H	1.785
S	2.106

Choose *True* or *False* for each inequality.

- **A** T > S ☐ True ☐ False
- **B** W < G ☐ True ☐ False
- **C** G > H ☐ True ☐ False
- **D** S < W ☐ True ☐ False
- **E** W > H ☐ True ☐ False

5 Which equation is true? Circle the letter for all that apply.

- **A** $61 \times 5 = 3,050 \div 10$
- **B** $381 \times 27 = 1,143 \div 9$
- **C** $8,054 \times 8 = 64,432$
- **D** $5,621 \times 42 = 236,082$

6   Ben is learning about place value in his math class.

Part A

Ben writes the number 74,443. The value of the digit 4 in the hundreds place is 10 times the value of the digit 4 in what place value?

Answer _____

Part B

Ben's teacher asks him to write a three-digit number that uses the digit 3 once and the digit 6 twice. The value of one 6 needs to be $\frac{1}{10}$ the value of the other 6. What number can Ben write?

Answer _____

7   Coach Miller is having a cookout at the park for his baseball team.

Part A

Coach Miller bought 5.15 pounds of ground beef to make burgers. The cost of ground beef is $3.40 per pound. What was the total cost for all of the ground beef?

Show your work.

Answer _____

Part B

Coach Miller is grilling 17 burgers. What is the cost per burger?

Show your work.

Answer _____

Performance Task

Answer the questions and show all your work on separate paper.

You have a movie theater gift card worth $40, so you invite a friend to go to the movies with you. Your friend challenges you to spend the exact value of the gift card. Find at least one way to do so by choosing from the items listed below.

Tickets	
2D movie	$7.25
3D movie	$8.50
Refreshments	
Popcorn	Small $3.25, Medium $5.50, and Large $7.75
Water	$2.50 per bottle
Snack Mix	$0.50 per ounce

Reflect on Mathematical Practices

After you complete the task, choose one of the following questions to answer.

1. **Persevere** What strategies did you use? If a strategy did not work, what did you do?

2. **Model** How did you use equations to solve this problem?

Sometimes, sharing can be easy. You might want to share a batch of 24 cookies equally with a friend. Splitting the batch into two groups will give you each 12 cookies. But you might decide that, since you baked the cookies, you should get $\frac{2}{3}$ of the batch. How many should you get? Can you also give your friend $\frac{2}{3}$ of the cookies? In order to solve this dilemma, you will need to know how to add fractions and multiply by a fraction.

In this unit, you will learn how to add, subtract, multiply, and divide fractions. You will also see how fractions can be used in many real-world situations.

✓ Self Check

Before starting this unit, check off the skills you know below. As you complete each lesson, see how many more you can check off!

I can:	Before this unit	After this unit
add and subtract fractions with unlike denominators, for example: $\frac{3}{5} + \frac{1}{4} = \frac{17}{20}$	☐	☐
estimate sums or differences of fractions, for example: $2\frac{3}{8} + 5\frac{1}{2}$ is a little less than 8	☐	☐
multiply fractions, for example: $\frac{2}{3} \times \frac{5}{6} = \frac{10}{18}$ or $\frac{5}{9}$	☐	☐
divide unit fractions, for example: $4 \div \frac{1}{7} = 28$	☐	☐

Lesson 10 Part 1: Introduction

Add and Subtract Fractions

In Grade 4, you learned that adding and subtracting fractions is similar to adding whole numbers. Take a look at this problem.

Emiliano needs $\frac{1}{2}$ cup of butter to make corn bread and $\frac{1}{4}$ cup of butter to make apple muffins. How many cups of butter does he need?

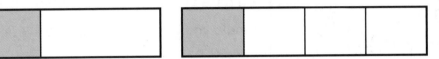

🔍 Explore It

Use the math you already know to solve the problem.

- Will Emiliano need more than 1 cup of butter or less than 1 cup of butter for the corn bread and the apple muffins? _____

- How do you know? _____

  _____

- Do $\frac{1}{2}$ and $\frac{1}{4}$ have like denominators? _____

- What is the least common multiple of 2 and 4? _____

- How do you find equivalent fractions? _____

  _____

- Write an equivalent fraction for $\frac{1}{2}$ using fourths.

  $$\frac{1}{2} = \frac{\square}{4}$$

- You now have the same size fraction of a cup. How many fourths of a cup of butter does Emiliano need?

  $\frac{1}{2} + \frac{1}{4} =$ _____ $+ \frac{1}{4} =$ _____; so he needs _____ cup of butter

Find Out More

To add fractions, the size of the parts that make up the whole must be the same. Because $\frac{1}{2}$ and $\frac{1}{4}$ are different-size parts, you rewrote $\frac{1}{2}$ as the equivalent fraction $\frac{2}{4}$. Since $\frac{1}{4}$ and $\frac{2}{4}$ are both fourths, you combined $\frac{2}{4}$ and $\frac{1}{4}$ to get the sum $\frac{3}{4}$.

The same idea works for subtracting fractions. Here is a similar problem: $\frac{3}{4} - \frac{1}{2}$.

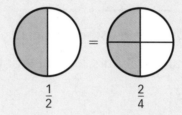

$$\frac{3}{4} \qquad \frac{1}{2} \qquad \frac{2}{4}$$

To subtract $\frac{2}{4}$ from $\frac{3}{4}$, you can take 2 shaded parts away from the 3 shaded parts. You have 1 shaded part left.

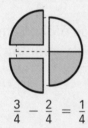

$$\frac{3}{4} - \frac{2}{4} = \frac{1}{4}$$

Before adding or subtracting fractions, the fractions must represent the same size part of a whole. To show this, the fractions must have the same denominator.

Reflect

1 Write a multiplication equation that shows how the denominators of $\frac{3}{4}$ and $\frac{1}{2}$ are related. Explain how this equation helps you write $\frac{1}{2}$ as an equivalent fraction with a denominator of 4.

_____

_____

_____

Read the problem below. Then explore different ways to add fractions with unlike denominators.

Jenna spent $1\frac{2}{3}$ hours mowing the back yard. After taking a break, she spent $\frac{3}{4}$ hour mowing the front yard. How much time did she spend mowing her whole yard?

🔍 Picture It

You can picture the fractions in the problem using models.

The shaded parts represent the back yard, $1\frac{2}{3}$ hours, and the front yard, $\frac{3}{4}$ hour.

$1\frac{2}{3}$ hours   + $\frac{3}{4}$ hour

Because the sections need to be divided into equal-sized parts to add, use dashed lines to divide the fraction models into 12 equal parts. This works because 12 is a common multiple of 3 and 4.

$1\frac{8}{12}$ hours   + $\frac{9}{12}$ hour

🔍 Model It

You can use a number line to add fractions.

The number line is divided into twelfths with a point at $1\frac{2}{3}$.

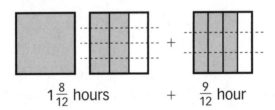

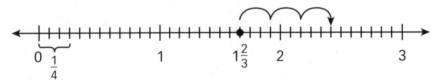

$\frac{1}{4} = \frac{3}{12}$, so $\frac{3}{4} = \frac{3}{12} + \frac{3}{12} + \frac{3}{12}$.

$\frac{3}{12} + \frac{3}{12} + \frac{3}{12} = \frac{9}{12}$

Start at $1\frac{2}{3}$ and jump right $\frac{9}{12}$.

Connect It

Now you will solve the problem from the previous page using equivalent fractions and addition.

2 Are $1\frac{2}{3}$ and $\frac{3}{4}$ made up of equal-sized parts? Justify your answer. _____

_____

3 Look at the models on the previous page. What is a common denominator of $1\frac{2}{3}$ and $\frac{3}{4}$? _____

4 You can find this common denominator without a model. Write a multiplication equation that shows how the denominators 3 and 4 are related to 12.

_____

5 Use this common denominator to find equivalent fractions for $1\frac{2}{3}$ and $\frac{3}{4}$.

$1\frac{2}{3} = 1$ _____ $\frac{3}{4} =$ _____

6 Using the equivalent fractions, what is the sum of $1\frac{2}{3}$ and $\frac{3}{4}$? _____

7 Explain how to add two fractions with unlike denominators. _____

_____

_____

Try It

Use what you just learned about adding fractions with unlike denominators to solve these problems. Show your work on a separate sheet of paper.

8 What is $1\frac{1}{6} + 2\frac{3}{8}$? _____

9 Hank practices $\frac{2}{5}$ of his spelling words on Monday. He practices another $\frac{1}{2}$ of his words on Tuesday. How much of his spelling list has Hank practiced so far? _____

Read the problem below. Then explore different ways to subtract fractions with unlike denominators.

Gavin's water bottle has $1\frac{3}{8}$ cups of water. He drinks $\frac{1}{2}$ cup. How much water is left in the bottle?

Picture It

You can use a picture to model subtracting fractions.

The water bottle is shaded to show that it has 1 cup $+ \frac{3}{8}$ cup of water in it. 1 cup is equivalent to $\frac{8}{8}$ cup. The bottle has 11 eighths shaded.

Gavin drinks $\frac{1}{2}$ cup. $\frac{1}{2}$ is equivalent to $\frac{4}{8}$ cup, so take away 4 shaded parts of the bottle. There are 7 parts of the bottle left with water in it.

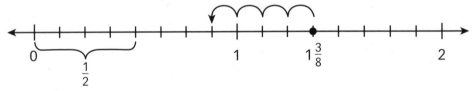

Model It

You can use a number line to model subtracting fractions.

The number line below is divided into $\frac{1}{8}$s with a point at $1\frac{3}{8}$.

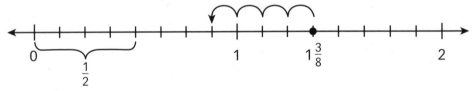

$\frac{1}{2}$ is equivalent to $\frac{4}{8}$. $\frac{4}{8}$ is four $\frac{1}{8}$ units on the number line. Start at $1\frac{3}{8}$ and jump left $\frac{4}{8}$.

Connect It

Now you will solve the problem from the previous page using equivalent fractions and subtraction equations.

10 Estimate the amount of water left in Gavin's bottle. _____

How did you arrive at your estimate? _____

_____

11 Look at Picture It and Model It on the previous page. Why was $\frac{1}{2}$ rewritten as $\frac{4}{8}$?

_____

_____

12 Use the number line on the previous page to rewrite $1\frac{3}{8}$ as a fraction greater than 1 and write a subtraction equation with equivalent fractions.

_____ − _____ = _____

13 Why was it helpful to rewrite $1\frac{3}{8}$ as a fraction greater than 1? _____

_____

14 Explain how to subtract two fractions with unlike denominators. _____

_____

_____

Try It

Use what you just learned about subtracting fractions with unlike denominators to solve these problems. Show your work on a separate sheet of paper.

15 What is $\frac{7}{8} − \frac{1}{2}$? _____

16 Emily's living room window is $2\frac{5}{6}$ feet wide. The window in her bedroom is $1\frac{1}{3}$ feet wide. How much wider is the living room window than her bedroom window? _____

Study the model below. Then solve problems 17–19.

I need to find a common denominator before I subtract fractions.

Student Model

Chapter 1 of Henry's book is $5\frac{2}{3}$ pages long. Chapter 2 is $8\frac{2}{5}$ pages long. How much longer is Chapter 2 than Chapter 1?

Look at how you could show your work using an equation.

$$5 + \left(\frac{2 \times 5}{3 \times 5}\right) = 5\frac{10}{15}$$

$$8 + \left(\frac{2 \times 3}{5 \times 3}\right) = 8\frac{6}{15}$$

$$8\frac{6}{15} = \left(7 + \frac{15}{15}\right) + \frac{6}{15} = 7\frac{21}{15}$$

$$7\frac{21}{15}$$
$$-\ 5\frac{10}{15}$$
$$\overline{2\frac{11}{15}}$$

Solution: $2\frac{11}{15}$ **pages**

🗨 Pair/Share

Explain why the model regrouped $8\frac{6}{15}$ as $7\frac{21}{15}$.

I think this sum is a little more than 3. I can use this estimate to check if my answer is reasonable.

17 What is $1\frac{1}{2} + 1\frac{2}{3}$?

Show your work.

🗨 Pair/Share

Explain why you chose the type of model used to solve this problem.

Solution: _____

18 Michael rode his bike $2\frac{2}{3}$ miles on Saturday. He rode another $1\frac{5}{6}$ miles on Sunday. How many miles did Michael ride his bike on both days combined?

Show your work.

How are the denominators 3 and 6 related?

Solution: _____

Pair/Share

How did you decide what operation to use to solve this problem?

19 Cara's bathroom floor has an area of $2\frac{2}{3}$ square yards. She lays down a rug that has an area of $1\frac{1}{4}$ square yards. What amount of floor is NOT covered by the rug? Circle the letter of the correct answer.

A 1 square yard

B $1\frac{1}{12}$ square yards

C $1\frac{5}{12}$ square yards

D $1\frac{3}{7}$ square yards

John chose **D** as the correct answer. How did he get that answer?

_____

_____

_____

_____

What equivalent mixed numbers could I subtract?

Pair/Share

Does a denominator of 7 make sense?

Solve the problems.

1 The model below represents the expression $1\frac{5}{8} + 2\frac{1}{3}$.

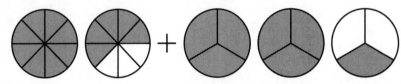

Which of the following could NOT be represented by the model?

A $1 + 2 + \frac{6}{11}$

B $1\frac{15}{24} + 2\frac{8}{24}$

C $\frac{39}{24} + \frac{56}{24}$

D $2 + 1 + \frac{23}{24}$

2 Mackenzie's footprint is $\frac{7}{12}$ foot long. Her dad's footprint is $1\frac{1}{6}$ feet long. Which equation can be used to find how much longer Mackenzie's dad's footprint is than Mackenzie's? Select *Yes* or *No* for each equation.

A $1\frac{2}{12} - \frac{7}{12} = \square$ ☐ Yes ☐ No

B $\frac{7}{12} - 1\frac{1}{6} = \square$ ☐ Yes ☐ No

C $1\frac{1}{6} - \frac{2}{3} = \square$ ☐ Yes ☐ No

D $\frac{14}{12} - \frac{7}{12} = \square$ ☐ Yes ☐ No

3 Find two fractions in the list below that can be added using the denominator 18. Write those two fractions in the box.

$\frac{1}{4}$ $\frac{5}{6}$ $\frac{7}{12}$ $\frac{1}{8}$ $\frac{4}{9}$

Like denominator = 18

4 Lucy is making a smoothie by following the recipe below.

> ## Sunshine Smoothie
>
> $1\frac{1}{3}$ cups banana
>
> $\frac{1}{2}$ cup yogurt
>
> 1 cup strawberries
>
> $\frac{3}{4}$ cup orange juice
>
> Place all ingredients in blender
> and blend until smooth.

Part A

Will this recipe make enough for Lucy and 3 friends to each have at least 1 cup of smoothie? Explain.

_____

_____

_____

Part B

How much smoothie remains after Lucy gives each of her friends $\frac{3}{4}$ cup of smoothie?

Show your work.

Answer _____ cups

Lesson 11   Part 1: Introduction 👥

Add and Subtract Fractions in Word Problems

CCSS
5.NF.A.2

Now that you can add and subtract fractions with different denominators, you can use this skill to solve word problems. Take a look at this problem.

Aleena has a 1-gallon watering can. She uses $\frac{3}{8}$ gallon to water her roses and $\frac{1}{3}$ gallon to water the geraniums. How much water did Aleena use to water both the roses and geraniums?

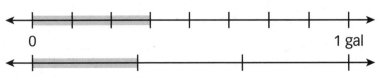

🔍 Explore It

Use the math you already know to solve the problem.

▪ Does Aleena use more than $\frac{1}{2}$ gallon or less than $\frac{1}{2}$ gallon of water? _____

▪ How do you know? _____

_____

▪ Estimate how much water Aleena used. _____

_____

▪ Write an equation with equivalent fractions to find the amount of water Aleena used.

_____

▪ Is this answer reasonable based on your estimate? Explain. _____

_____

Find Out More

The number line below shows the location of **benchmark fractions** between 0 and 2. You can use common fractions to estimate sums and differences.

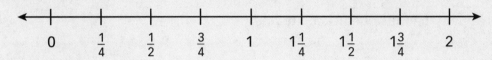

$$0 \quad \frac{1}{4} \quad \frac{1}{2} \quad \frac{3}{4} \quad 1 \quad 1\frac{1}{4} \quad 1\frac{1}{2} \quad 1\frac{3}{4} \quad 2$$

There are different ways to estimate the sums or differences of fractions. The examples below show two ways to think about fractions and find estimates for the amount of water Aleena used to water her flowers.

$$\frac{3}{8} + \frac{1}{3} = ?$$

Student A

"$\frac{1}{3}$ and $\frac{3}{8}$ are both less than $\frac{1}{2}$, or $\frac{4}{8}$. So the sum must be less than 1."

Student B

"$\frac{3}{8}$ is a little greater than $\frac{1}{4}$. $\frac{1}{3}$ is a little greater than $\frac{1}{4}$. If I add $\frac{1}{4} + \frac{1}{4}$, I estimate the sum to be greater than $\frac{1}{2}$."

Reflect

1 Both estimates above model correct thinking. Which estimate makes more sense to you? Why?

_____

_____

_____

Read the problem below. Then explore different ways to estimate and solve problems with fractions.

Frankie purchases a $3\frac{1}{2}$-pound bag of chicken. He uses $1\frac{1}{3}$ pounds of chicken for fajitas. How many pounds of chicken are left?

Picture It

You can picture the problem using a fraction strip.

The fraction strip below represents $3\frac{1}{2}$ pounds of chicken. It is separated into sections representing the $1\frac{1}{3}$ pounds used for fajitas and the unused amount.

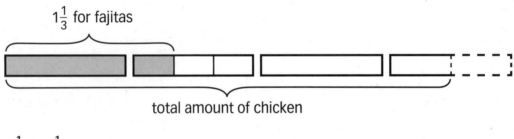

$1\frac{1}{3}$ for fajitas

total amount of chicken

$3\frac{1}{2} - 1\frac{1}{3}$

Model It

You can model the problem with a number line.

Since $2 \times 3 = 6$, the fractions in the problem, $3\frac{1}{2}$ and $1\frac{1}{3}$, can be represented with a common denominator of 6.

The number line below is divided into sixths. It shows starting with a total of $3\frac{1}{2}$, with two jumps to the left representing the $1\frac{1}{3}$ pounds of chicken used.

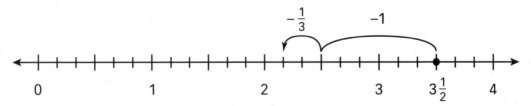

$-\frac{1}{3}$ -1

0   1   2   3 $3\frac{1}{2}$ 4

$3\frac{1}{2} = 3\frac{3}{6}$ and $1\frac{1}{3} = 1\frac{2}{6}$

$3\frac{3}{6} - 1\frac{2}{6}$

✎ **Connect It**

Now you will estimate and then solve the problem from the previous page using benchmark fractions and an equation.

2 Identify the closest half on either side of $1\frac{1}{3}$

$1\frac{1}{3}$ is greater than _____ and less than _____.

3 Why are halves a good choice for benchmark fractions for $1\frac{1}{3}$?

_____

4 The difference $3\frac{1}{2}$ minus $1\frac{1}{3}$ must be between _____ and _____.
Estimate $3\frac{1}{2} - 1\frac{1}{3}$ and explain your estimate.

_____

5 Find the actual difference. _____

There are _____ pounds of chicken remaining.

6 Is this a reasonable answer based on your estimate? Explain. _____

_____

7 Explain how you can check if a fraction sum or difference is reasonable.

_____

_____

✎ **Try It**

Use what you just learned about estimating with benchmark fractions to solve this problem. Show your work on a separate sheet of paper.

8 Tim's bean sprout grew $3\frac{3}{8}$ inches. Teegan's bean sprout grew $2\frac{3}{4}$ inches. How many more inches did Tim's bean sprout grow than Teegan's? First, estimate the difference and explain your reasoning. Then find the actual difference. _____

_____

Study the model below. Then solve problems 9–11.

The blue field of stars on an American flag has an area of $1\frac{3}{5}$ square yards. The red stripes have a combined area of $2\frac{3}{10}$ square yards. What is the difference between the area of the blue field of stars and the area of the red stripes?

Look at how you could show your work using fraction strips.

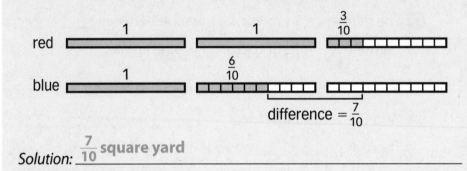

red   1   1 $\frac{3}{10}$

blue   1 $\frac{6}{10}$

difference $= \frac{7}{10}$

Solution: $\frac{7}{10}$ **square yard**

What common denominator was used to subtract these fractions?

Pair/Share

Do you agree with the estimate in the problem? Why or why not?

---

9 Parker mixes $3\frac{1}{2}$ ounces of blue paint with $1\frac{2}{5}$ ounces of yellow paint to create green for the leaves of a tree. How many ounces of green paint did Parker create?

Estimate, and then compute. Explain how you know your result is reasonable.

Show your work.

Will there be a little more than $4\frac{1}{2}$ ounces or a little less than $4\frac{1}{2}$ ounces of green paint?

Pair/Share

Was your estimate more than or less than the actual answer? By how much?

Solution: _____

_____

10 Jose's football weighs $\frac{7}{8}$ pound. His football helmet weighs $5\frac{1}{6}$ pounds. Estimate how much more the helmet weighs. Explain your estimate.

Solution: _____

_____

What benchmark fractions could I use to estimate the difference in weight?

🔲 **Pair/Share**

How does an estimate help you tell if your answer is reasonable?

11 Which is a reasonable estimate for the difference, $5\frac{1}{2} - 3\frac{5}{9}$? Circle the letter of the correct answer.

A between $\frac{1}{2}$ and 1

B between 1 and $1\frac{1}{2}$

C between $1\frac{1}{2}$ and 2

D between 2 and $2\frac{1}{2}$

Elise chose **D** as the correct answer. How did she get that answer?

_____

_____

_____

_____

How can I use benchmark fractions to estimate the difference?

🔲 **Pair/Share**

Does Elise's answer make sense?

Solve the problems.

1 William compares monthly rainfall amounts for the summer months using the table below.

Month	Monthly Rainfall
June	$3\frac{3}{10}$ inches
July	$3\frac{3}{4}$ inches
August	$3\frac{1}{2}$ inches

About how much more rain fell in July than in June?

A $\frac{1}{4}$ inch

B $\frac{1}{2}$ inch

C 1 inch

D $1\frac{1}{2}$ inches

2 Several expressions are shown. Decide if the value of each expression is less than $1\frac{1}{2}$, between $1\frac{1}{2}$ and 2, or greater than 2. Write each expression in the correct category in the chart.

$$2\frac{1}{2} - 1\frac{1}{8} \qquad 1\frac{5}{11} + \frac{3}{4} \qquad 3\frac{4}{5} - 1\frac{1}{3} \qquad \frac{3}{8} + \frac{9}{10}$$

Less than $1\frac{1}{2}$	Between $1\frac{1}{2}$ and 2	Greater than 2

3   The table below shows the thickness of coins.

Coin	Thickness
quarter	$1\frac{3}{4}$ millimeters
dime	$1\frac{7}{20}$ millimeters
nickel	$1\frac{19}{20}$ millimeters
penny	$1\frac{1}{2}$ millimeters

Hailey stacks a dime on top of a penny. She estimates the thickness of the two coins to be less than 3 millimeters.

Write a symbol (<, >, or =) in the box to make the statement true. Then use the statement to tell whether Hailey's estimate is correct.

$$1\frac{1}{2} + 1\frac{7}{20} \quad \boxed{} \quad 1\frac{1}{2} + 1\frac{1}{2}$$

Is Hailey's estimate correct? _____

4   Jimmy says $3\frac{4}{9} - 2\frac{5}{6}$ is $1\frac{1}{3}$.

Part A

Without finding the actual difference, explain why Jimmy's difference is or is not reasonable.

_____

_____

Part B

Find the actual difference.

Show your work.

Solution _____

 **Self Check** *Go back and see what you can check off on the Self Check on page 85.*

Lesson 12 Part 1: Introduction

Fractions as Division

CCSS
5.NF.B.3

You know that division is used for equal sharing, and fractions represent a number of equal parts. In this lesson, you will learn how division and fractions are related. Take a look at this problem.

Mrs. Tatum needs to share 4 ounces of red paint equally among 5 art students. How much red paint will each student get?

1 ounce   1 ounce   1 ounce   1 ounce

🔍 Explore It

Use the math you already know to solve the problem.

▢ Start with 1 ounce of paint. What fraction is represented by 1 ounce of paint shared equally among 5 students?

1 ounce of paint shared equally among 5 students = _____ ounce per student.

▢ Look at the model above. Write a multiplication expression that represents a student getting $\frac{1}{5}$ of each of 4 ounces of paint. _____

▢ What fraction is represented by the product? _____

▢ 4 ounces of paint ÷ 5 students = _____ ounce of paint per student.

Find Out More

Each student will get $\frac{1}{5}$ ounce of paint if 1 ounce of paint is shared among 5 students.

1 ounce ÷ 5 students = $\frac{1}{5}$ ounce per student

What if Mrs. Tatum wants to share 8 ounces of paint equally among the 5 students? How much will each student get? You can look at this quotient two ways.

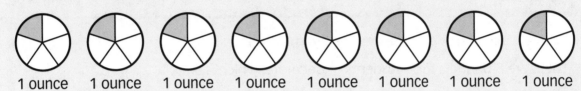

1 ounce   1 ounce   1 ounce   1 ounce   1 ounce   1 ounce   1 ounce   1 ounce

8 ounces ÷ 5 students = $\frac{8}{5}$ ounces per student

Here is another way to look at this. Each student will receive 1 full ounce of paint because there are 5 students. This leaves 3 ounces remaining.

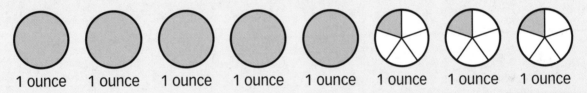

1 ounce   1 ounce   1 ounce   1 ounce   1 ounce   1 ounce   1 ounce   1 ounce

3 ounces ÷ 5 students = $\frac{3}{5}$ ounce per student

If 8 ounces of paint is shared equally among 5 students, each student will receive 1 ounce plus $\frac{3}{5}$ ounce of paint.

8 ounces ÷ 5 students = $1\frac{3}{5}$ ounces per student

Reflect

1 Using the situation in the problem on the previous page, what quotient could be represented by $\frac{2}{5}$? Describe it in words.

_____

_____

_____

Read the problem below. Then explore different ways to understand fractions as quotients.

Jared, Monica, and Heather have 5 banners to decorate for the student council. If they share the work equally, how much will each student decorate?

Picture It

You can use a model to represent the quotient.

There are 5 banners for 3 students to decorate, which is $5 \div 3$.

If they share the work equally, each student can decorate $\frac{1}{3}$ of each banner.

J   M   H

$\frac{1}{3} \times 5 = \frac{5}{3}$

$5 \div 3 = \frac{5}{3}$

Model It

You can use a number line to represent the quotient.

The number line is numbered from 0 to 5 because there are 5 banners. It is divided into thirds because each student can decorate one third of each banner.

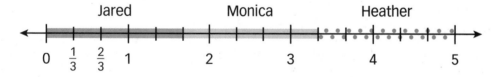

5 divided into 3 equal sections is equivalent to five thirds, $\frac{5}{3}$.

Connect It

Now you will solve the problem from the previous page by thinking about division as equal sharing.

2 How many thirds of a banner are there to decorate in 5 banners? _____ thirds

3 How many thirds of a banner will each student decorate if the thirds are shared equally? _____ thirds

Write this as a fraction. _____ of a banner

Here is another way to think of the problem.

4 How many whole banners can each student decorate? _____

How many banners remain after these are removed? _____

If 5 banners are shared equally by 3 students, there will be _____ whole banner per student and _____ banners remaining.

5 How much of 2 remaining banners will each student decorate? _____

5 banners ÷ 3 students = _____ whole and _____ banner per student

Write this as a mixed number. _____ banners

6 Write two division equations, one using the fraction and one using the mixed number, to represent the quotient.

_____

7 Thinking about division, what does a fraction mean? _____

_____

Try It

Use what you just learned about fractions as quotients to solve these problems. Show your work on a separate piece of paper.

8 Five friends are equally sharing 3 packs of football cards. How much of a pack will each friend get? _____

9 Mary made 18 ounces of applesauce. She evenly portions the applesauce among 4 containers. How many ounces of applesauce are in 1 container? Write a division expression to represent the problem and solve. _____

Study the model below. Then solve problems 10–12.

Student Model

Luke, Carter, and Ava want to divide 2 quarts of juice evenly among them. How many quarts of juice will each of them get?

Look at how you could show your work using a model.

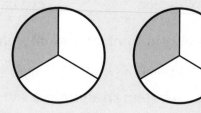

$$\frac{1}{3} \times 2 = \frac{2}{3}$$

Solution: $\frac{2}{3}$ quart

2 quarts are shared by 3 friends, so I know that each friend will have less than 1 quart of juice. That means the quotient is a fraction.

💬**Pair/Share**

Model the problem for 3 quarts of juice divided evenly among Luke, Carter, Ava, and Ava's little brother.

---

10 Erica has 7 square feet of garden space to plant carrots, beans, peppers, and lettuce. If she gives each vegetable an equal amount of space, how much space does each vegetable get?

Show your work.

Solution: _____

Each vegetable will get at least 1 square foot of garden space. How will the rest of the space be divided up?

💬**Pair/Share**

What are some ways you can check your solution?

11 Daniel needs to make 6 pizza crusts. He has 20 ounces of dough and wants to make all the crusts the same size. He weighs a portion of dough for 1 crust on a scale. Between what 2 whole numbers of ounces did it weigh?

Show your work.

How many whole ounces of dough will each crust get? What will happen with the remaining ounces?

Solution: _____

Pair/Share

Create a different division story to represent $\frac{20}{6}$.

12 Jonas is doing a science experiment with his class. The teacher has 21 ounces of pond water to equally share with 10 pairs of students. How much pond water will Jonas and his science partner receive? Circle the letter of the correct answer.

A $\frac{10}{21}$ oz

B $1\frac{1}{10}$ oz

C 2 oz

D $\frac{21}{10}$ oz

Olivia chose **A** as the correct answer. How did she get that answer?

_____

_____

_____

_____

About how much water will each pair of students receive? Will it be more or less than 2 ounces?

Pair/Share

Does Olivia's answer make sense?

Solve the problems.

1 Teddy makes 32 ounces of hot cocoa. He needs to pour equal amounts of cocoa into 5 cups. Each cup will contain between —

A   3 and 4 ounces.

B   4 and 5 ounces.

C   5 and 6 ounces.

D   6 and 7 ounces.

2 Pierce has 8 minutes to complete 10 math problems. How many minutes does he have to spend on each problem?

A $\frac{2}{10}$ minute

B $\frac{8}{10}$ minute

C $\frac{10}{8}$ minutes

D $1\frac{2}{8}$ minutes

3 Dani needs 8 equal sections from a board that is 13 meters long. Which expression represents 1 section of the board? Select *Yes* or *No* for each expression.

A $1\frac{5}{8}$ ☐ Yes   ☐ No

B $\frac{8}{13}$ ☐ Yes   ☐ No

C $\frac{13}{8}$ ☐ Yes   ☐ No

D $8 \div 13$ ☐ Yes   ☐ No

E $13 \times \frac{1}{8}$ ☐ Yes   ☐ No

4   Which situation is represented by $\frac{25}{9}$? Circle the letter for all that apply.

   A   Melanie equally shares 25 meters of paper to create 9 murals.

   B   Quill gives away 9 baseball cards from a pack of 25 cards.

   C   George invites 25 kids and 9 adults to his birthday party.

   D   Becca creates 9 rows with 25 buttons each.

   E   Joe makes 9 equal servings from a 25-ounce bag of peanuts.

5   Paco is trying to explain to his friend that $7 \div 2 = \frac{7}{2}$.

Part A

   Draw a model or number line showing $7 \div 2 = \frac{7}{2}$.

Part B

   Explain the equivalence of $7 \div 2$ and $\frac{7}{2}$ using words.

   _____

   _____

✓ **Self Check**   *Go back and see what you can check off on the Self Check on page 85.*

Lesson 13   Part 1: Introduction
Understand Products of Fractions

What does it mean to multiply a fraction by a whole number?

The ruler below shows three $\frac{1}{2}$-inch segments. This is represented by $3 \times \frac{1}{2}$.

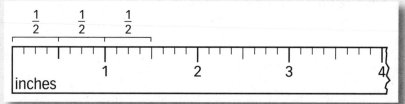

You have learned many different ways to think about fractions and also about multiplication. Here are some other ways to think about $3 \times \frac{1}{2}$ inch:

three $\frac{1}{2}$-inch sections is $\frac{3}{2}$ inches

three $\frac{1}{2}$-inch sections is 1 whole inch plus $\frac{1}{2}$ inch, or $1\frac{1}{2}$ inches

$\frac{3}{2}$ inches is 3 times as long as $\frac{1}{2}$ inch

🔍 Think   What does it mean to multiply a whole number by a fraction?

The ruler below shows a 3-inch segment divided into 2 equal parts. That's the same as multiplying 3 by $\frac{1}{2}$.

This is represented by $\frac{1}{2} \times 3$.

> **Shade $\frac{1}{2}$ of 3 inches on the ruler.**

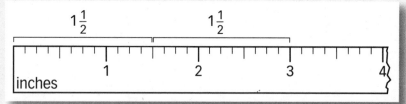

Here are some ways to think about $\frac{1}{2} \times 3$:

When 3 is divided into 2 equal parts. $\frac{1}{2} \times 3$ is one part.

When 3 is divided into 2 equal parts, each part is $1\frac{1}{2}$ or $\frac{3}{2}$.

$\frac{1}{2} \times 3 = 1\frac{1}{2}$

🔍 **Think** What happens when a fraction is multiplied by a fraction?

Find $\frac{1}{4}$ of a $\frac{1}{2}$-inch line segment,

or $\frac{1}{4} \times \frac{1}{2}$.

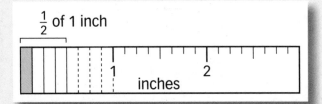

$\frac{1}{2}$ of 1 inch

If I say "find one fourth of," it means to divide by 4 or multiply by $\frac{1}{4}$.

The ruler shows that $\frac{1}{2}$ inch is half of the whole 1 inch.

To find $\frac{1}{4}$ of $\frac{1}{2}$ inch, you divide the half inch into 4 equal parts.

Remember that one half inch is already part of the whole 1 inch. Divide the other half-inch into 4 equal parts, and the whole will have 8 equal parts. So, $\frac{1}{4}$ of $\frac{1}{2}$ inch is 1 of 8 parts of the whole 1 inch: $\frac{1}{8}$ inch.

What if the problem is to find $\frac{3}{4}$ of a $\frac{1}{2}$ inch line segment?

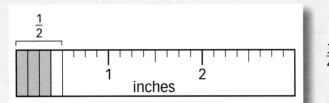

$\frac{3}{4} \times \frac{1}{2}$

Above, you found that $\frac{1}{4}$ of $\frac{1}{2}$ inch is $\frac{1}{8}$ inch. This problem asks you to find three $\frac{1}{4}$s of $\frac{1}{2}$ inch.

If $\frac{1}{4} \times \frac{1}{2}$ is $\frac{1}{8}$, then $\frac{3}{4}$ of $\frac{1}{2}$ is three $\frac{1}{8}$s, or $\frac{3}{8}$. So, $\frac{3}{4} \times \frac{1}{2} = \frac{3}{8}$.

✏️ **Reflect**

1 Based on the two problems above, what do you expect is the product of $\frac{2}{4} \times \frac{1}{2}$? Explain.

_____

_____

_____

🔍 Explore It

Find the product of $\frac{3}{4} \times \frac{2}{3}$ with an area model.

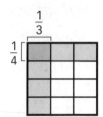

2   Look at the first model. Each column is what fraction of the whole? _____

     Each row is what fraction of the whole? _____

3   The dark green part shows $\frac{1}{4}$ of $\frac{1}{3}$. How many parts are in the whole? _____

     So, $\frac{1}{4} \times \frac{1}{3}$ is what fraction of the whole? _____

4   Look at the second model. Two columns are what fraction of the whole? _____

     Three rows are what fraction of the whole? _____

5   The dark green parts show $\frac{3}{4}$ of $\frac{2}{3}$. What fraction of the whole is $\frac{3}{4} \times \frac{2}{3}$? _____

6   What is the product of $\frac{3}{4} \times \frac{2}{3}$? _____

💬 Talk About It

Complete these problems as a group.

7   Use the area model above to fill in the products in the table below.

$\frac{1}{4} \times \frac{1}{3} =$		$\frac{2}{4} \times \frac{1}{3} =$		$\frac{3}{4} \times \frac{1}{3} =$		$\frac{4}{4} \times \frac{1}{3} =$	
$\frac{1}{4} \times \frac{2}{3} =$		$\frac{2}{4} \times \frac{2}{3} =$		$\frac{3}{4} \times \frac{2}{3} =$		$\frac{4}{4} \times \frac{2}{3} =$	

8   Look at the numerators of each factor pair. How do these numbers relate to the numerator of the product? Look at the denominators and answer the same question. What pattern do you see? _____

_____

_____

✎ Try It Another Way

Work with your group to connect the model to the multiplication expression.

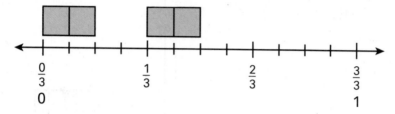

$\frac{2}{4} \times \frac{2}{3}$

9 Each third on the number line is divided into how many equal parts? _____

Each of these parts is what fraction of the whole? _____

10 How many fourths of the first $\frac{1}{3}$ are shaded? _____

How many fourths of the second $\frac{1}{3}$ are shaded? _____

11 How many twelfths of the whole are shaded? _____

12 Explain how the model shows $\frac{2}{4} \times \frac{2}{3}$. What is the product? _____

_____

_____

Connect It

Talk through these problems as a class. Then write your answers below.

13 **Describe:** Tell what multiplication problem the model shows.
Explain why. _____

_____

_____

_____

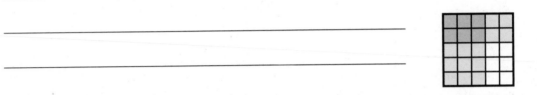

14 **Explain:** Landon said that $\frac{2}{3} \times \frac{1}{6} = \frac{5}{6}$. Tell how Landon got his product, and then

explain how to find the correct product. _____

_____

_____

_____

_____

15 **Create:** Create a multiplication table for the unit fractions from $\frac{1}{2}$ to $\frac{1}{4}$. Identify two

patterns that can be seen in the table.

×	$\frac{1}{2}$	$\frac{1}{3}$	$\frac{1}{4}$
$\frac{1}{2}$			
$\frac{1}{3}$			
$\frac{1}{4}$			

_____

_____

Put It Together

16 Use what you have learned to complete this task.

A Use a piece of paper. Fold it in half, then fold it in half again. Continue folding the paper in half. As you do, fill in the blanks to tell what fraction of the whole each equal part is.

$$\frac{1}{2} \times 1 = \underline{\hspace{2cm}}$$

$$\frac{1}{2} \times \frac{1}{2} = \underline{\hspace{2cm}}$$

$$\frac{1}{2} \times \underline{\hspace{2cm}} = \underline{\hspace{2cm}}$$

$$\frac{1}{2} \times \underline{\hspace{2cm}} = \underline{\hspace{2cm}}$$

B Write the products as the terms of a pattern. Then look at the denominators of the fractions. Each time you multiply by $\frac{1}{2}$, what happens to the denominator?

_____

_____

Without folding the paper, what do you think the next fraction in the pattern will be? Why?

_____

_____

C Now look at the sizes of the equal parts of the folded paper. Each time you fold the paper in half, what happens to the size of the parts?

_____

_____

In Lesson 13, you learned about multiplying fractions. Now you will use area models to multiply fractions. Take a look at this problem.

Mr. Thompson creates a square on his whiteboard with $\frac{5}{10}$-meter sides. He uses the space to post a weekly puzzle. How many square meters of whiteboard space does he use for the weekly puzzle?

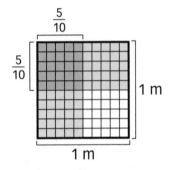

Explore It

Use the math you already know to solve the problem.

- How do you find the area of the large square in the model? Explain.

  _____

- How do you find the area of the shaded square? _____

- The shaded square is 5 units wide and 5 units long. How many square units is this?

  _____

- What is the total number of small squares in the large square? _____

- What fraction of the whole square is the shaded part? _____

- The area of the shaded square is _____ square meter.

©Curriculum Associates, LLC   Copying is not permitted.

Find Out More

The equation and model show the area of the puzzle square in the problem on the previous page.

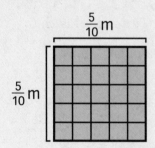

$$\frac{5}{10} \text{ m} \times \frac{5}{10} \text{ m} = \frac{25}{100} \text{ sq m}$$

Think about the factors. The numerators represent the number of units (5 × 5).

The denominators represent the size of the units $\left(\frac{1}{10} \text{ meter} \times \frac{1}{10} \text{ meter.}\right)$

Here is another way to look at multiplying $\frac{5}{10}$ by $\frac{5}{10}$.

You can write $\frac{5}{10}$ as a $5 \times \frac{1}{10}$. Use the expression $5 \times \frac{1}{10}$ to rewrite $\frac{5}{10} \times \frac{5}{10}$.

$$\frac{5}{10} \times \frac{5}{10} = \left(5 \times \frac{1}{10}\right) \times \left(5 \times \frac{1}{10}\right)$$

You can change the grouping in multiplication without changing the product.

$$\frac{5}{10} \times \frac{5}{10} = (5 \times 5)\left(\frac{1}{10} \times \frac{1}{10}\right)$$

$$\frac{5}{10} \times \frac{5}{10} = 25 \times \frac{1}{100}, \text{ or } \frac{25}{100}$$

Reflect

1 Refer to the diagrams to explain why multiplying the numerators tells you the number of parts in the product.

_____

_____

_____

Read the problem below. Then explore different ways to understand multiplying two unit fractions.

Titus has a square sheet of paper measuring 1 foot on each side. He folds the paper in half vertically and then folds it into fourths horizontally. Titus unfolds the paper and colors each part a different color. What is the area of each part?

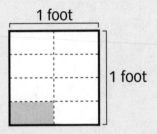

1 foot

1 foot

Picture It

You can understand the problem by picturing parts of the unfolded paper.

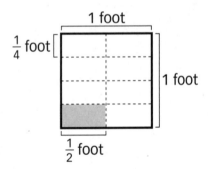

1 foot

$\frac{1}{4}$ foot

1 foot

$\frac{1}{2}$ foot

The folding created 8 equal sections. Each section is $\frac{1}{8}$ of the whole. Each section is $\frac{1}{2}$ foot wide and $\frac{1}{4}$ foot long.

Model It

You can model the problem with an equation.

Each equal part of the paper has a length of $\frac{1}{2}$ foot and width of $\frac{1}{4}$ foot.

$$\text{area} = \frac{1}{2} \text{ foot} \times \frac{1}{4} \text{ foot}$$

$$\frac{1}{2} \text{ foot} \times \frac{1}{4} \text{ foot} = \frac{1 \times 1}{2 \times 4} \text{ square foot}$$

Connect It

Now you will solve the problem from the previous page by connecting the model to the equation.

2 Explain why each part of the paper is $\frac{1}{2}$ foot long. _____

_____

_____

3 Explain why each part of the paper is $\frac{1}{4}$ foot wide. _____

_____

_____

4 What expression do you use to find the area of 1 part of the paper? _____

5 Multiply the denominators of these fractions. How does the product relate to the size of the units compared to the size of the whole model? _____

_____

6 Multiply the numerators of these fractions. How does the product relate to the number of shaded parts of the model? _____

_____

7 Explain how to find the area of one part of the piece of paper.

_____

_____

_____

Try It

Use what you just learned about multiplying unit fractions to solve this problem. Show your work on a separate sheet of paper.

8 What is the area of a paper strip with a width of $\frac{1}{3}$ yard and length of $\frac{1}{6}$ yard?

_____

Read the problem below. Then explore different ways to understand multiplying fractions greater than 1.

> A state flag stamp has a width of $\frac{3}{4}$ inch and length of $\frac{3}{2}$ inches. What is the area of the stamp in square inches?

Picture It

You can picture the problem using the area of a rectangle.

The first area model shows $\frac{1}{4}$ inch $\times$ $\frac{1}{2}$ inch $= \frac{1}{8}$ square inch. The second model uses the same $\frac{1}{8}$ square inch parts to show an area that is $\frac{3}{4}$ inch $\times$ $\frac{3}{2}$ inches.

$$\frac{1}{4} \times \frac{1}{2}$$

$$\frac{3}{4} \times \frac{3}{2}$$

Model It

You can model the problem with an equation.

The dimensions of the stamp are $\frac{3}{4}$ inch and $\frac{3}{2}$ inches, so multiply the fractions to find the area.

$$\text{area} = \frac{3}{4} \times \frac{3}{2} = \frac{3 \times 3}{4 \times 2}$$

Connect It

Now you will solve the problem from the previous page by connecting the model to the equation.

9 Look at the area model for $\frac{3}{4} \times \frac{3}{2}$. Explain why each part shows $\frac{1}{8}$ square inch.

_____

10 What do the 3 columns of the model together stand for? _____

What do the 3 rows together stand for? _____

11 How many eighths are shaded dark green? _____ eighths

Write this as a fraction greater than 1. _____

12 Now look at the equation in Model It. Multiply the numerators, multiply the denominators, and write the fraction. How does this product compare with the one shown by the area model?

_____

_____

13 How do you multiply fractions greater than 1?

_____

_____

_____

Try It

Use what you just learned about multiplying fractions to solve this problem. Show your work on a separate sheet of paper.

14 Bernice's math workbook is $\frac{2}{3}$ foot wide and $\frac{5}{6}$ foot long. What is the area of a page in the workbook? _____

Study the model below. Then solve problems 15–17.

Student Model

Rachel is designing a newspaper ad. The ad will include a piece of art whose dimensions are $\frac{5}{8}$ inch long and $\frac{1}{2}$ inch wide. How many square inches of space does Rachel have to work with?

Look at how you could show your work using an area model.

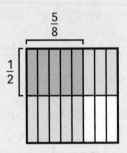

$$\frac{5}{8} \times \frac{1}{2} = \frac{5 \times 1}{8 \times 2}$$

$$\frac{5 \times 1}{8 \times 2} = \frac{5}{16}$$

Solution: $\frac{5}{16}$ square inch

$\frac{1}{8}$ inch $\times \frac{1}{2}$ inch is $\frac{1}{16}$ square inch. How many sixteenths square inches are shown in the model?

📣Pair/Share

How can you write $\frac{5}{8} \times \frac{1}{2}$ as a product of unit fractions and whole numbers?

How can I represent a fractional side length with an area model?

📣Pair/Share

Find the area of a $\frac{3}{4}$ yard by $\frac{6}{5}$ yard rectangle. How is the model different?

---

15 What is the area of a rectangle with a length of $\frac{1}{2}$ yard and a width of $\frac{11}{6}$ yards? Write an equation to represent your solution.

Show your work.

Solution: _____

16 Brent is designing a poster that has an area of 1 square foot. He is going to paste a photo collage on a section of the poster that is $\frac{1}{3}$ foot wide and $\frac{3}{5}$ foot long. What part of a square foot will the photo collage cover?

Show your work.

If I draw a square to represent a square foot, what can I do to it to represent thirds and fifths?

Solution: _____

**Pair/Share**

Write an equation to represent your model. Explain the meaning of the numerators.

17 What is the area of the square below? Circle the letter of the correct answer.

$\frac{6}{7}$ yd

$\frac{6}{7}$ yd

A $\frac{36}{49}$ square yard

B $\frac{12}{14}$ square yard

C $\frac{49}{36}$ square yards

D $\frac{12}{7}$ square yards

Ollie chose **D** as the correct answer. How did he get that answer?

_____

_____

Think about the size of the two fractions. Will the product of the fractions be greater than 1 or less than 1?

Pair/Share

Does Ollie's answer make sense?

Solve the problems.

1 The square below represents 1 square unit.

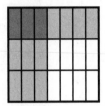

Which expression represents the area of the dark gray section?

A $\frac{7}{3} \times \frac{3}{1}$ square units

B $\frac{3}{7} \times \frac{1}{3}$ square units

C $\frac{1}{7} \times \frac{1}{3}$ square units

D $\frac{7}{3} \times \frac{1}{3}$ square units

2 Fill in the missing numbers to make the equation true. Then complete the area model to check your answer.

$$\frac{1}{6} \times \frac{\boxed{}}{\boxed{}} = \frac{1}{24}$$

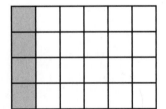

3 Which product could you find by shading the model below? Circle the letter for all that apply.

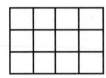

A $\frac{3}{4} \times \frac{1}{3}$

B $\frac{1}{3} \times \frac{1}{6}$

C $\frac{2}{3} \times \frac{1}{4}$

D $\frac{5}{3} \times \frac{1}{4}$

E $\frac{3}{4} \times \frac{3}{4}$

4   Draw an area model to represent the expression $\frac{5}{4}$ inches $\times \frac{4}{5}$ inch.

5   Show how to find the area of the rectangle in problem 4.

_____

_____

6   Find the dimensions of a different rectangle that has the same area as the rectangle in problem 4. Show how you know the area is the same.

_____

_____

✓ **Self Check**   *Go back and see what you can check off on the Self Check on page 85.*

Understand Multiplication as Scaling

What does scaling mean?

Think of how you use words and phrases such as "double," "triple," "half of," or "take one tenth." These words and phrases describe changing the size of a quantity, or scaling. Stretching and shrinking are two different ways to scale a quantity.

The table below shows some ways that a quantity of 6 can be scaled.

	Words	Symbols
stretching	6 doubled is 12.	$2 \times 6 = 12$
	6 tripled is 18.	$3 \times 6 = 18$
shrinking	Half of 6 is 3.	$\frac{1}{2} \times 6 = 3$
	A tenth of 6 is $\frac{6}{10}$.	$\frac{1}{10} \times 6 = \frac{6}{10}$

Think How can you use models to show what scaling means?

Here is a rectangle with an area of 6 square units.

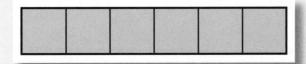

> **Circle the numbers that describe how the rectangle is being stretched or shrunk.**

The model for 2×6 has an area that is double the size of the original rectangle.

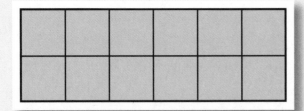

The model for $\frac{1}{2} \times 6$ has an area that is half the size of the original rectangle.

Think How does the size of the factors affect the product?

Products aren't always greater than their factors. The table below shows products of different factors times 6.

×	$\frac{1}{10}$	$\frac{1}{3}$	$\frac{1}{2}$	$\frac{5}{6}$	1	$\frac{4}{3}$	2	$2\frac{1}{2}$	3
6	$\frac{6}{10}$	2	3	5	6	8	12	15	18

Look at the products that are less than 6, then look at those that are greater than 6. What do you notice about the factors?

Notice that the products are sometimes less than 6, sometimes greater than 6, and sometimes equal to 6.

What do the products that are less than 6 have in common? The other factor is less than 1. If you multiply 6 by a factor less than 1, the product will be less than 6.

What do the products that are greater than 6 have in common? The other factor is greater than 1. If you multiply 6 by a factor greater than 1, the product will be greater than 6.

The product of a factor times 6 is equal to 6 when the other factor equals 1 or a number that is equivalent to 1.

Reflect

1 Describe the products you can get if you multiply 8 by a factor less than 1. Describe the products you can get if you multiply 8 by a factor greater than 1. Give some examples that justify your answers.

_____

_____

_____

Explore It

A number line can help you see what happens when a fraction is multiplied by a factor less than 1.

2 You can show $\frac{1}{3} \times \frac{3}{4}$ on a number line. If you break up $\frac{3}{4}$ into 3 equal parts, each part is $\frac{1}{4}$.

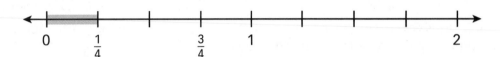

$$\frac{1}{3} \times \frac{3}{4} = \underline{\hspace{2cm}}$$

Is the product less than, greater than, or equal to $\frac{3}{4}$? _____

3 Show $\frac{2}{3} \times \frac{3}{4}$ on a number line. If you break up $\frac{3}{4}$ into 3 equal parts, each part is $\frac{1}{4}$. Since you multiply by $\frac{2}{3}$, you need 2 of those parts. Shade and label $\frac{2}{3}$ of $\frac{3}{4}$.

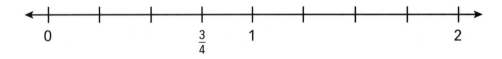

$$\frac{2}{3} \times \frac{3}{4} = \underline{\hspace{2cm}}$$

Is the product less than, greater than, or equal to $\frac{3}{4}$? _____

4 You multiplied $\frac{3}{4}$ by two different factors. What is true about both of those factors? What happens when you multiply a given fraction by a factor less than 1?

_____

_____

Talk About It

A number line can also help you see what happens when a fraction is multiplied by a factor greater than 1.

5 Shade the number line to show $\frac{4}{3} \times \frac{3}{4}$.

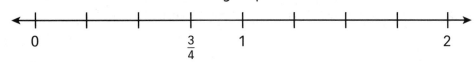

$\frac{4}{3} \times \frac{3}{4} =$ _____

Is the product less than, greater than, or equal to $\frac{3}{4}$? _____

6 Shade and label the number line to show $\frac{7}{3} \times \frac{3}{4}$.

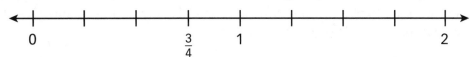

$\frac{7}{3} \times \frac{3}{4} =$ _____

Is the product less than, greater than, or equal to $\frac{3}{4}$? _____

7 Think about how each of your answers compared to $\frac{3}{4}$. What can you say about the product of a given fraction and a factor greater than 1?

_____

Try It Another Way

Explore multiplying $\frac{3}{4}$ by a fraction using an area model.

The model to the right represents $\frac{3}{4}$.

8 Show $\frac{1}{2} \times \frac{3}{4}$ using the area model.

9 $\frac{1}{2} \times \frac{3}{4} =$ _____

10 Is the product less than, greater than, or equal to $\frac{3}{4}$? _____

11 Could you have answered problem 11 without drawing a model? Explain.

_____

Connect It

Talk through these problems as a class, then write your answers below.

12 Analyze: Use reasoning to order the following expressions from least to greatest. Don't calculate any of the products. Explain your reasoning.

$$\frac{7}{9} \times 348{,}980 \qquad \frac{12}{11} \times 348{,}980 \qquad \frac{50}{50} \times 348{,}980$$

_____

_____

_____

13 Explain: Gillian said that the product of a given number and a fraction is always less than the given number. Explain what is wrong with Gillian's statement and give an example that does not follow her rule.

_____

_____

_____

_____

14 Compare: Represent the expression $\frac{4}{4} \times \frac{8}{5}$ with a model. Write a sentence comparing the product with $\frac{8}{5}$. Explain your reasoning.

_____

_____

Put It Together

15 You can compare the size of a product to the size of the factors in a multiplication equation if you know whether the factors are greater than, less than, or equal to 1.

A Write a multiplication equation (different from one in this lesson) where the product is greater than both of the factors. Draw a model to support your answer.

_____

_____

B Write a multiplication equation (different from one in this lesson) where the factors are both fractions and the product is less than both of the factors. Draw a model to support your answer.

_____

_____

C Write a multiplication sentence (different from one in this lesson) where the product is equal to one of the factors.

_____

_____

Lesson 16   Part 1: Introduction

Multiply Fractions in Word Problems

CCSS

5.NF.B.6

Now that you have learned how to multiply fractions, take a look at this problem.

> Grayson lives $\frac{4}{5}$ mile from the park. He has already walked $\frac{3}{4}$ of the way there.
> How far has Grayson walked?

 Explore It

Use the math you already know to solve the problem.

- You can draw a model to help you solve the problem. Locate a point on the number line below to show how far Grayson lives from the park.

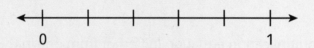

- Label the point to show the distance to the park.

- Shade the segment that shows one fourth of the way to the park. One fourth of the way to the park is _____ of a mile. Label this distance.

- Two fourths of the way to the park is _____ of a mile.

- Three fourths of the way to the park is _____ of a mile.

- Explain how you can use the model to show how far Grayson has already walked.

_____

_____

Find Out More

The distance you need to find is a fraction of a fraction: $\frac{3}{4}$ of $\frac{4}{5}$ mile.

Finding $\frac{3}{4}$ of a number is the same as multiplying the number by $\frac{3}{4}$.

$$\frac{3}{4} \text{ of } \frac{4}{5} \text{ means } \frac{3}{4} \times \frac{4}{5}$$

To multiply two fractions, multiply the numerators to get the numerator of the product, and then multiply the denominators to get the denominator of the product.

$$\frac{3}{4} \times \frac{4}{5} = \frac{3 \times 4}{4 \times 5} = \frac{12}{20}$$

The fraction $\frac{12}{20}$ is equivalent to $\frac{3}{5}$. To find equivalent fractions, multiply or divide the numerator and denominator of the fraction by the same number.

$$\frac{12}{20} = \frac{12 \div 4}{20 \div 4} = \frac{3}{5}$$

Both methods give you the same answer: Grayson has walked $\frac{3}{5}$ mile.

Your answer is reasonable, since it is less than $\frac{4}{5}$. When you multiply $\frac{4}{5}$ by a factor less than 1, the product should be less than $\frac{4}{5}$.

Reflect

1 Which strategy, drawing a model or writing an equation, made more sense to you for solving this problem? Why?

_____

_____

_____

Read the problem below. Then explore different ways to understand how to find a fraction of a fraction.

Brandon's mother left $\frac{3}{4}$ of a pizza on the counter. If Brandon eats $\frac{2}{3}$ of it, how much of the original whole pizza did Brandon eat?

 **Picture It**

You can draw a picture to help you understand the problem.

Show $\frac{3}{4}$ of a pizza.

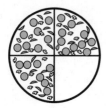

Since Brandon eats $\frac{2}{3}$ of what is left, shade in 2 of the 3 pieces that are left. You can see from the shaded parts how much of the original whole pizza Brandon ate.

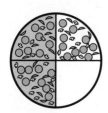

Model It

You can write an equation to help you understand the problem.

You need to find a fraction of a fraction: $\frac{2}{3}$ of $\frac{3}{4}$ of a pizza.

$\frac{2}{3}$ of $\frac{3}{4}$ means $\frac{2}{3} \times \frac{3}{4}$

$\frac{2}{3} \times \frac{3}{4} = \frac{2 \times 3}{3 \times 4}$

Connect It

Now you will solve the problem from the previous page comparing both strategies.

2 Look at the picture. Why did you shade 2 of the 3 parts of the pizza?

_____

3 How much of the whole pizza did Brandon eat? Explain your reasoning.

_____

_____

4 Look at the model. How do you know that you should multiply $\frac{2}{3} \times \frac{3}{4}$?

_____

_____

5 What is $\frac{2 \times 3}{3 \times 4}$? _____

Is this answer the same as your answer to problem 3 above? Explain.

_____

6 What are some strategies you can use to solve a word problem that involves multiplying fractions? _____

_____

_____

Try It

Use what you just learned about finding products of fractions to solve these problems. Show your work on a separate sheet of paper.

7 Lewis rode his bike 10 miles. He stopped for a break $\frac{2}{5}$ of the way into his ride. How many miles did Lewis ride before he stopped for a break? _____

8 Jamie worked $\frac{5}{6}$ hour filing papers for her mother. She listened to music for $\frac{2}{5}$ of the time she spent filing. How much time did Jamie spend listening to music?

_____

Read the problem below. Then explore different ways to understand multiplying fractions and mixed numbers.

Janie has $2\frac{3}{4}$ yards of yellow fabric. She uses $\frac{1}{2}$ of the fabric to make a blanket for her new baby cousin. How many yards of fabric did Janie use for the blanket?

 **Picture It**

You can use an area model to help you understand the problem.

The darker shading of the area model shows half of $2\frac{3}{4}$.

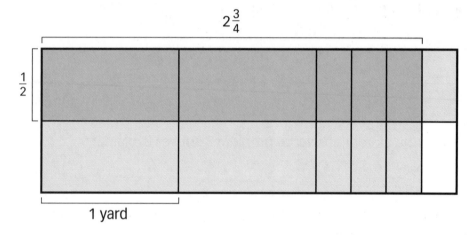

$2\frac{3}{4}$

$\frac{1}{2}$

1 yard

Model It

You can write an equation to help you understand the problem.

You can write $2\frac{3}{4}$ as a fraction.

$$2\frac{3}{4} = 2 + \frac{3}{4}$$
$$= \frac{8}{4} + \frac{3}{4}$$
$$= \frac{11}{4}$$

You need to find a fraction of a fraction: $\frac{1}{2}$ of $\frac{11}{4}$ yards of fabric.

$\frac{1}{2}$ of $\frac{11}{4}$ means $\frac{1}{2} \times \frac{11}{4}$

$$= \frac{1 \times 11}{2 \times 4}$$

Connect It

Now you will solve the problem from the previous page comparing the two strategies.

9 Does Janie use more or less than $2\frac{3}{4}$ yards of fabric for the blanket? Explain.

_____

_____

10 How many yards of fabric did Janie use? _____ Explain how you can use the picture to answer the question. _____

_____

11 How do you know that you should multiply to solve the problem? _____

_____

12 How can you multiply $2\frac{3}{4}$ by $\frac{1}{2}$? _____

_____

13 What is $\frac{1}{2} \times 2$? _____ What is $\frac{1}{2} \times \frac{3}{4}$? _____

Add the two products. _____ + _____ = _____

Is this answer the same as your answer to question 10 above? _____

14 Suppose Janie had $2\frac{1}{4}$ yards of fabric. Explain how you could find how many yards of fabric she used for the blanket. _____

_____

Try It

Use what you just learned about multiplying mixed numbers to solve this problem. Show your work on a separate sheet of paper.

15 Izzy has a length of $3\frac{1}{2}$ yards of sidewalk to decorate for her school festival. She decides to decorate $\frac{3}{5}$ of her sidewalk space with a drawing of the school. How many meters of space does Izzy use to draw the school? _____

Study the solution below. Then solve problems 16–18.

The student wrote and solved an equation to solve the problem.

Student Model

Chris is $4\frac{1}{4}$ feet tall. His mom is $1\frac{1}{2}$ times as tall. How tall is Chris's mom?

Look at how you can solve this problem using an equation.

$$4\frac{1}{4} \times 1 = 4\frac{1}{4}$$

$$4\frac{1}{4} \times \frac{1}{2} = 4 \times \frac{1}{2} + \frac{1}{4} \times \frac{1}{2} = 2 + \frac{1}{8}$$

$$4\frac{1}{4} + 2 + \frac{1}{8} = 6\frac{1}{4} + \frac{1}{8} = 6\frac{2}{8} + \frac{1}{8} = 6\frac{3}{8}$$

Solution: $6\frac{3}{8}$ feet

Pair/Share

How does the answer compare to $4\frac{1}{4}$ feet?

How do I know what operation to use to solve this problem?

16 Josh exercises at the gym $3\frac{3}{4}$ hours a week. He spends $\frac{2}{5}$ of his time lifting weights. How many hours a week does Josh spend lifting weights at the gym?

Show your work.

Pair/Share

What is a reasonable estimate for the number of hours Josh lifts weights each week?

Solution: _____

17 A field is in the shape of a rectangle $\frac{5}{6}$ mile long and $\frac{3}{4}$ mile wide. What is the area of the field?

Show your work.

What model can I use to help understand this problem?

Solution: _____

🗨**Pair/Share**

Can you solve this problem in another way?

18 Ari had $\frac{3}{4}$ of a bag of popcorn. His friends ate $\frac{1}{2}$ of his popcorn. What fraction of the whole bag of popcorn did Ari's friends eat? Circle the letter of the correct answer.

A $\frac{1}{4}$

B $\frac{3}{8}$

C $\frac{5}{4}$

D $\frac{3}{2}$

Kayla chose **A** as the correct answer. How did she get that answer?

_____

_____

_____

_____

What equation can I write to solve this problem?

🗨**Pair/Share**

Does Kayla's answer make sense?

Solve the problems.

1 On Sunday, Kristen bought a carton of 24 bottles of water.

- On Monday, Kristen drank $\frac{1}{6}$ of the bottles in the carton.

- On Tuesday, Kristen drank $\frac{1}{4}$ of the bottles that remained in the carton after Monday.

Which picture represents the number of bottles of water remaining in the carton after Kristen drank the water on Tuesday?

A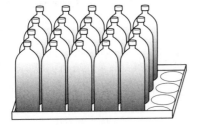

C

B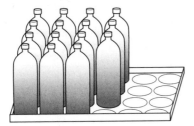

D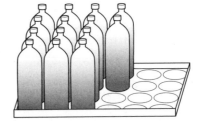

2 Milo's pancake recipe makes 9 servings. It calls for $\frac{3}{4}$ cup milk. Milo wants to make 6 servings. How much milk will he need?

☐ cup

©Curriculum Associates, LLC   Copying is not permitted.

3 Look at the rectangle below.

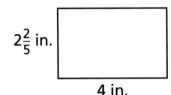

$2\frac{2}{5}$ in.

4 in.

What is the area of the rectangle? ☐ or ☐ square inches

4 Lily designed the letters of her name on the computer and printed them on paper. The table below shows the width and height of the printed letters.

Letter	Width	Height
L	$2\frac{1}{2}$"	4"
I	$1\frac{3}{4}$"	4"
Y	$1\frac{2}{3}$"	4"

She used a copier to change the size of the letters by a factor of $\frac{3}{4}$. Make a table to show the new dimensions of each letter.

Show your work.

✓ **Self Check**   *Go back and see what you can check off on the Self Check on page 85.*

Lesson 17   Part 1: Introduction 👥

Understand Division with Unit Fractions

How is dividing with fractions related to multiplying with fractions?

You know that multiplication and division are related. Dividing 8 by 4, for example, gives the same result as multiplying 8 by $\frac{1}{4}$.

$$8 \div 4 = 2$$

$$8 \times \frac{1}{4} = 2$$

Dividing with **unit fractions** works the same way. You can solve a fraction-division problem with multiplication.

🔍 Think   What does dividing a unit fraction by a whole number mean?

Mrs. Cook wants to share $\frac{1}{4}$ pound of fish equally among 3 cats.

That means she needs to divide $\frac{1}{4}$ into 3 equal parts. You can draw an area model to represent the problem.

> **Circle the multiplication equation that solves the division situation.**

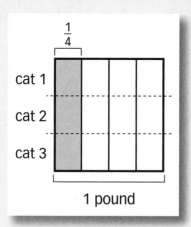

$$\frac{1}{4} \div 3 = \frac{1}{12}$$

If $\frac{1}{4}$ pound of fish is divided into 3 equal parts, each cat will receive $\frac{1}{3}$ of the $\frac{1}{4}$ pound of fish.

$$\frac{1}{3} \times \frac{1}{4} = \frac{1}{12}$$

Think What does dividing a whole number by a unit fraction mean?

Mr. Putnam cuts a 3-foot rope into $\frac{1}{4}$-foot sections.

To figure out how many sections he will get, Mr. Putnam thinks, "How many fourths are in 3?"

You can draw a number line to represent the 3 feet of rope. There are three 1-foot sections.

Look at the answer to this division problem. It is greater than the number I started with!

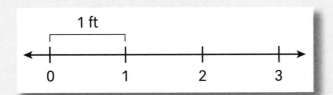

You can mark fourths on the number line to represent $\frac{1}{4}$ foot. You can see there are twelve $\frac{1}{4}$-foot sections in 3 feet.

$$3 \div \frac{1}{4} = 12$$

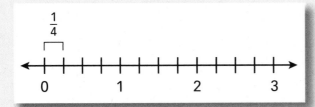

You can also write a multiplication equation to show how many fourths are in 3. There are 4 fourths in each whole foot. To find the number of fourths in 3 feet, you can multiply.

$$3 \times 4 = 12$$

When you divide 3 by $\frac{1}{4}$, you are dividing 3 into parts smaller than 1, so there will be more than 3 of those parts.

Reflect

1 Explain what it means to divide 5 by $\frac{1}{4}$.

_____

_____

🔍 **Explore It**

Explore dividing a whole number by a unit fraction with the problem below.

Jemma made 5 cups of pancake batter. She uses a scoop measuring $\frac{1}{3}$ cup to pour batter onto the skillet to make large pancakes. How many pancakes can Jemma make?

The 5 rectangles below represent the 5 cups of pancake batter.

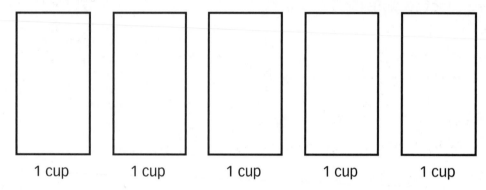

1 cup   1 cup   1 cup   1 cup   1 cup

2 You need to find out how many _____ there are in _____.

3 The scoop holds $\frac{1}{3}$ cup of batter. How many scoops are in 1 cup? _____

4 Divide each of the 5 rectangles into sections to show your answer to problem 3.

5 How many scoops are in 5 cups? _____

6 $5 \div \frac{1}{3} =$ _____

7 What multiplication equation will also solve this problem? _____

8 How is 5×3 related to $5 \div \frac{1}{3}$? _____

_____

Talk About It

Solve the problems below as a group.

Suppose Jemma wanted to divide $\frac{1}{3}$ cup of pancake batter to make 4 mini pancakes.

What fraction of a cup of batter will each pancake get?

9 The rectangle to the right shows 1 cup divided into 3 equal sections. How much does each section represent?

_____

10 Shade $\frac{1}{3}$ of the rectangle to show $\frac{1}{3}$ cup.

11 You need to divide $\frac{1}{3}$ cup equally to make 4 pancakes.

Divide each third of the rectangle vertically into 4 equal parts. Then shade $\frac{1}{4}$ of the rectangle to show 1 of the 4 pancakes.

12 The overlapping section shows the fraction of a cup of batter that each pancake will

get. What is this fraction? _____

13 $\frac{1}{3} \div 4 =$ _____

14 What multiplication equation also solves this problem of $\frac{1}{4}$ of $\frac{1}{3}$? _____

15 How is $\frac{1}{3} \div 4$ related to $\frac{1}{3} \times \frac{1}{4}$? _____

_____

Try It Another Way

Explore dividing by a unit fraction using a common denominator.

Another way to think about dividing fractions is to write equivalent fractions with a

common denominator. When both fractions have the same denominator, dividing is

easy. What is $5 \div \frac{1}{2}$?

16 Write 5 as a fraction with a denominator of 2. _____

17 Divide $\frac{10}{2}$ into equal groups of $\frac{1}{2}$. How many groups can you make? _____

18 $5 \div \frac{1}{2} =$ _____

Connect It

Talk through these problems as a class, then write your answers below.

19 **Compare:** Draw a model to represent $\frac{1}{4} \div 4$ and a model to represent $\frac{1}{4} \times \frac{1}{4}$. Explain the relationship between the two expressions.

_____

20 **Analyze:** Helena said that $12 \div \frac{1}{3}$ is 4. Draw a model and use words to explain why Helena's statement is not reasonable.

_____

21 **Justify:** Show that $\frac{1}{2} \div 3 = \frac{1}{6}$ by using a model. Explain why the answer is less than the number you started with.

_____

_____

Put It Together

22 Use what you have learned to complete this task.

Choose one of the following problems to solve. Circle the problem you choose.

> Drew wants to run at least 6 miles this month. He plans to run $\frac{1}{4}$ mile each day. How many days will it take Drew to run 6 miles?

> Maya made $\frac{1}{2}$ quart of strawberry jam. She plans to share it equally among 4 friends. How much jam will each friend get?

A Draw a model to represent the problem.

B Write a division equation and a multiplication equation that represent the problem.

_____

_____

Lesson 18   Part 1: Introduction

Divide Unit Fractions in Word Problems

Now that you understand what it means to divide with unit fractions, take a look at this problem.

> Micah is running a 6-mile race. There are water stops every $\frac{1}{2}$ mile, including at the 6-mile finish line. How many water stops will there be?

🔍 Explore It

Use the math you already know to solve this problem.

- You want to find how many groups of $\frac{1}{2}$ there are in 6. Write a division expression that represents the problem. _____

- You can draw a model to help you solve the problem. Label the number line below from 0 to 6.

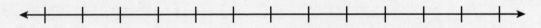

- Draw points on the number line to show the location of all the water stops.

- How many $\frac{1}{2}$s are in 1? _____

- How many $\frac{1}{2}$s are in 6? _____

- Explain how you can use the number line to find the number of water stops there will be. _____

_____

_____

🔍 Find Out More

This problem can be solved in many different ways.

Another way to show $6 \div \frac{1}{2}$ is by drawing a model. You can draw 6 rectangles to represent the 6 miles.

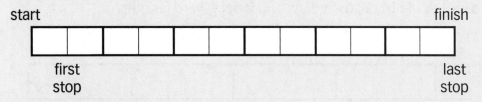

start   finish

Show and count the halves.

start   finish

first   last
stop   stop

There are 12 water stops.

You can also use common denominators to divide 6 by $\frac{1}{2}$. Consider these questions:

How many wholes are in 12?
How many groups of ten are in 12 tens?
How many groups of one hundred are in 12 hundreds?
How many groups of one tenth are in 12 tenths?
How many groups of one half are in 12 halves?

✏️ Reflect

1 What if there are water stops every $\frac{1}{4}$ mile, including the finish line? Explain how you could solve this problem.

_____

_____

_____

Read the problem below. Then explore different ways to understand dividing a fraction to solve word problems.

> Piper used $\frac{1}{5}$ yard of ribbon to create a border around a triangle. If the sides of the triangle are all the same length, how much ribbon did she use for each side?

Picture It

You can draw a picture to help understand the problem.

Draw a 1-yard length of ribbon, then draw and label $\frac{1}{5}$-yard lengths.

$\frac{1}{5}$

1 yard

Divide each $\frac{1}{5}$-yard length into 3 equal parts.

$\frac{1}{5}$

| side 1 | side 2 | side 3 | | | | | | | | | | | | |

1 yard

Model It

You can use a model to help understand the problem.

Draw and shade $\frac{1}{5}$ of a rectangle.

$\frac{1}{5}$

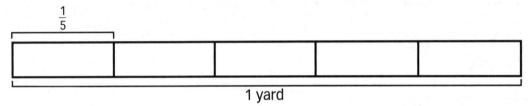

Divide the rectangle into 3 equal parts, then shade one of the thirds of the shaded $\frac{1}{5}$.

$\frac{1}{5}$

side 1
side 2
side 3

Connect It

Now you will solve the problem from the previous page using your understanding of fractions and the models.

2 Look at Picture It on the previous page. What information in the problem does the first picture show?

_____

3 Why does the second picture show each bar divided into 3 parts?

_____

4 When you divide $\frac{1}{5}$ meter into 3 equal parts, how long is each part? _____ meter

How do you know? _____

_____

5 How much ribbon did Piper use for each side of the triangle? _____

6 What division expression represents this problem? _____

7 What is $\frac{1}{5} \div 3$? _____

8 Describe how Model It on the previous page shows dividing a fraction by a whole number. _____

_____

_____

Try It

Use what you just learned about dividing fractions to solve this problem. Show your work on a separate sheet of paper.

9 Tate has $\frac{1}{4}$ of a pizza. He wants to share the pizza equally with a friend. How much of the original whole pizza will each of them get? Draw a model and write an equation for your answer.

_____

Read the problem below. Then explore different ways to understand dividing a whole number by a fraction.

Alex makes 2 pounds of bread dough. He needs to separate the dough into $\frac{1}{4}$-pound loaves for the oven. How many loaf pans will Alex need to bake all the loaves at the same time?

 **Picture It**

You can draw a model to help understand the problem.

Draw 2 rectangles to represent the 2 pounds of bread dough.

Show dividing each pound into fourths.

 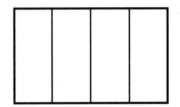

Model It

You can use a number line to help understand the problem.

Draw a number line and label it to show the 2 pounds of bread dough.

Mark the number line to show dividing into fourths.

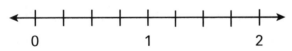

🔍 Connect It

Now you will solve the problem from the previous page using the models and equations.

10 Write a division expression that represents the problem. _____

11 How many fourths are in one whole? _____

How many fourths are in two wholes? _____

12 Use this information to solve the problem.

Using words:

There are _____ fourths in 2.

Using numbers:

$2 \div \frac{1}{4} =$ _____

13 What multiplication equation could you write to check your answer? _____

14 Describe a strategy you can use to divide a whole number by a unit fraction.

_____

_____

✏️ Try It

Use what you just learned about dividing whole numbers by fractions to solve this problem. Show your work on a separate sheet of paper.

15 Stacy has 4 sheets of paper to make cards. Each card requires $\frac{1}{2}$ sheet of paper. How many cards can Stacy make? Choose a strategy to solve the problem. Then explain why you chose that strategy.

_____

_____

Study the model below. Then solve problems 16–18.

The student used a model to visualize the problem.

Sierra has 3 empty pages for photos in an album. Each photo uses $\frac{1}{6}$ of a page. How many photos can Sierra put on the empty pages?

Look at how you could show your work using rectangles.

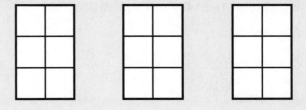

6 photos will fit on one page, so 18 photos will fit on 3 pages.

Solution: ___18 photos___

Pair/Share

What related equations can you write to represent the problem?

Can I draw a model to help understand the problem?

16 Corrine picked $\frac{1}{4}$ gallon of blackberries. She separated the berries equally into 4 containers. What fraction of a gallon is in each container?

Show your work.

Pair/Share

How will the answer compare to $\frac{1}{4}$ gallon?

Solution: _____

17 Cooper's USB drive is $\frac{1}{2}$ full with 5 video files. Each video file is the same size. What fraction of the USB drive does 1 video file use?
Show your work.

How could I represent this problem using an equation?

Solution: _____

Pair/Share

How can you check your answer?

18 Devonte is creating note cards to help him study for a history test. He fills 2 full sides of a sheet of paper and uses $\frac{1}{8}$ of a side for each major event he needs to study. Which expression shows the number of major events Devonte needs to study for the test? Circle the letter of the correct answer.

A $2 \times \frac{1}{8}$

B $2 \div \frac{1}{8}$

C $\frac{1}{8} \times 2$

D $\frac{1}{8} \div 2$

Barry chose **D** as the correct answer. How did he get that answer?

_____

_____

_____

_____

Is this problem like any problem I've seen before?

Pair/Share

Does Barry's answer make sense?

Solve the problems.

1   Elise picks 6 pounds of apples. She uses $\frac{1}{2}$ pound of apples to make 1 container of applesauce. How many containers of applesauce can Elise make?

     A   12 containers

     B $6\frac{1}{2}$ containers

     C $5\frac{1}{2}$ containers

     D   3 containers

2   Students are running in a relay race. Each team will run a total of 3 miles. Each member of a team will run $\frac{1}{3}$ of a mile.

     How many students will a team need to complete the race? Circle the correct number below.

            $\frac{1}{9}$ 3   9   12   36

     You may use the number line to help find your answer.

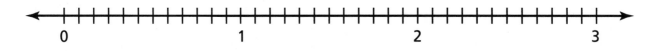

3 Mr. Bernstein will cut 8 pies into pieces that are each $\frac{1}{6}$ pie. After he cuts the 8 pies, how many pieces will Mr. Bernstein have? ☐ pieces

4 Marina has a pattern to make bows that requires $\frac{1}{4}$ yard of ribbon for each bow.

Part A

Fill in the table to show how many bows she can make from a given length of ribbon.

Yards of Ribbon	Number of Bows
1	
2	
3	
4	

Part B

Use words or an equation to describe a rule to find the number of bows Marina can make if you know how many yards of ribbon she has.

_____

Part C

Use your rule to find how many bows Marina can make if she has 18 yards of ribbon.

Answer _____ bows

 **Self Check** *Go back and see what you can check off on the Self Check on page 85.*

Solve the problems.

1 What is the area of the rectangle shown below?

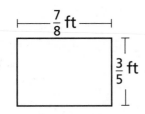

$\frac{7}{8}$ ft

$\frac{3}{5}$ ft

A $\frac{40}{21}$ square feet

B $\frac{10}{13}$ square foot

C $\frac{24}{35}$ square foot

D $\frac{21}{40}$ square foot

2 Look at the equations below. Choose *True* or *False* for each equation.

A $3\frac{4}{5} + 6\frac{2}{10} = 10$

☐ True   ☐ False

B $22\frac{7}{9} - 16\frac{1}{4} = 6\frac{19}{36}$

☐ True   ☐ False

C $\frac{2}{3} \times \frac{1}{6} = \frac{4}{6}$

☐ True   ☐ False

D $6 \div \frac{1}{5} = \frac{6}{5}$

☐ True   ☐ False

3 Classify each product below as less than $\frac{3}{7}$, equal to $\frac{3}{7}$, or greater than $\frac{3}{7}$ by writing each expression in the correct box.

$\frac{3}{7} \times \frac{1}{10}$ $\frac{3}{7} \times \frac{9}{4}$ $\frac{3}{7} \times 2$

$\frac{3}{7} \times \frac{2}{3}$ $\frac{3}{7} \times 1\frac{1}{8}$ $\frac{3}{7} \times \frac{5}{5}$

Less than $\frac{3}{7}$	Equal to $\frac{3}{7}$	Greater than $\frac{3}{7}$

4 Look at each fraction. Can it be placed in the box to make a true inequality? Select *Yes* or *No* for fractions A–C.

$$\frac{4}{11} \times \boxed{} < \frac{4}{11}$$

A $\frac{5}{3}$ ☐ Yes   ☐ No

B $\frac{3}{3}$ ☐ Yes   ☐ No

C $\frac{1}{3}$ ☐ Yes   ☐ No

5 How many peanuts will each person get if 3 people share $\frac{1}{5}$ pound of peanuts equally?

Part A

Write and solve a division equation to represent the problem.

Show your work.

Answer _____ pound

Part B

Write a multiplication equation that explains why your division equation solved the problem.

Answer _____

6 Two students painted murals on canvas for a school play.

Part A

José painted a square-shaped mural. The length of each side of the canvas is $1\frac{1}{3}$ yards.

What is the area of the mural in square yards?

◻ square yards

Part B

Lori painted a rectangular mural with the same area as José's mural. Her mural was not square-shaped.

What could be the dimensions of Lori's mural, in yards?

Length = ◻ yards   Width = ◻ yards

Performance Task

Answer the questions and show all your work on separate paper.

The Drama Club is painting sets for their next play. Blue and green paint is on sale at the hardware store, so the students have sketched the design for a set that will use only those two paint colors. How much of each color will they need to buy in order to paint the set?

left side	center	right side
turquoise	$\frac{3}{4}$ blue	turquoise
	$\frac{1}{4}$ green	10 ft
18 ft	24 ft	18 ft

Notes

1 pint turquoise $= \frac{2}{3}$ pint green and $\frac{1}{3}$ pint blue

1 pint of paint covers about 40 square feet

Reflect on Mathematical Practices

After you complete the task, choose one of the following questions to answer.

1. **Persevere** What was your first step in solving this problem?

2. **Model** How did you use fractions to help you solve this problem?

Sometimes, it doesn't matter in which order you complete the steps in a problem. If you are topping a mushroom, pepperoni, pepper, and onion pizza, you could mix the vegetables together and put them on first. Then you could top the pizza with pepperoni. Or you could put on a layer of pepperoni and then put on your vegetable mixture. Either way, you have made a tasty pizza. If you are given the math problem "double 8 + 12 then add 43," the order in which you complete the steps is very important. The expressions $2 \times 8 + 12 + 43$ and $2 \times (8 + 12) + 43$ are solved using different steps and have different values.

In this unit, you will write and find the value of numerical expressions. You will also look for number patterns in data and create a model of the data on a line graph.

✓ Self Check

Before starting this unit, check off the skills you know below. As you complete each lesson, see how many more you can check off!

I can:	Before this unit	After this unit
evaluate expressions, for example: $48 \div (6 + 10) = 3$	☐	☐
write expressions, for example: "subtract 5 from 12, then multiply by 4" can be written as $(12 - 5) \times 4$	☐	☐

find the relationship between two sequences, for example:
        sequence 1: 0, 2, 4, 6, 8, . . .
        sequence 2: 0, 8, 16, 24, 32, . . .
Each term in sequence 2 is 4 times the corresponding term in sequence 1.
	☐	☐

create ordered pairs for two sequences and graph the relationship on the coordinate plane, for example: ordered pairs for sequence 1 and 2 above are (0, 0), (2, 8), (4, 16), (6, 24), (8, 32)	☐	☐

Lesson 19   Part 1: Introduction 👥

Evaluate and Write Expressions

CCSS

5.OA.A.1
5.OA.A.2

You know about the order of operations. Now you will see how using parentheses in an expression can change the value of the expression. Take a look at this problem.

> Maria and her friend go to a movie. At the snack stand, they each get a drink for $5 and popcorn for $8. Maria pays for her friend. How much does Maria pay altogether?

🔍 Explore It

Use the math you already know to solve the problem.

- What operation do you use to find the cost of a drink and popcorn for one person?

  _____

- Write an expression for the cost of a drink and popcorn for one person. _____

- How does the cost for two people compare to the cost for one person?

  _____

- Julie writes that the cost for two people is $2 \times 5 + 8$ which equals $18. How did Julie get her answer?

  _____

- Is the cost for two people to have a drink and popcorn equal to $18? _____

- Explain how you can get the cost for two people. What do you need to do first?

  _____

  _____

- How much does Maria pay for a drink and popcorn for two people? _____

Find Out More

$2 \times 5 + 8$ is an **expression**. To **evaluate** an expression means to find its value.

To evaluate $2 \times 5 + 8$, you first multiply 2×5 and then add 8.

In the problem on the previous page, Julie first needs to find the cost of a drink and popcorn for one person. Then she can multiply that by 2 to find the cost of a drink and popcorn for two people.

Since she needs to add first, she uses **parentheses**. To show adding $5 + 8$ first and then multiplying by 2, you write $2 \times (5 + 8)$ or $(5 + 8) \times 2$.

Here are some examples of grouping symbols.

Parentheses	$2 \times (5 + 8)$	Add $5 + 8$ first because it is in parentheses. Then multiply by 2.
Fraction Bar	$\dfrac{2 + 8}{11 - 6}$	The fraction bar groups the numerator separately from the denominator. Add $2 + 8$ first, then subtract $11 - 6$. Then, if you need to, divide.

When Julie wrote the expression $2 \times 5 + 8$, she didn't get the right result because she didn't put parentheses around $5 + 8$ to show that she needed to find that sum first.

You can think of an expression like $2 \times (5 + 8)$ as "add 5 and 8, then multiply by 2," or "2 times the sum of 5 and 8." Think of the problem on the previous page as "twice as much as the cost to buy a drink and popcorn for one person."

Reflect

1 Explain how you can recognize groupings and what you should do when you see them.

_____

_____

_____

_____

Read the problem below. Then explore how to evaluate expressions that use grouping symbols.

Twenty-four students went on a field trip to the aquarium. There were also 8 adults on the trip. The expression $0.5 \times (24 + 8)$ represents the cost to buy everyone a 50-cent dolphin eraser to remember the trip. What is the total cost of the erasers?

 **Picture It**

You can use a picture to help understand the problem.

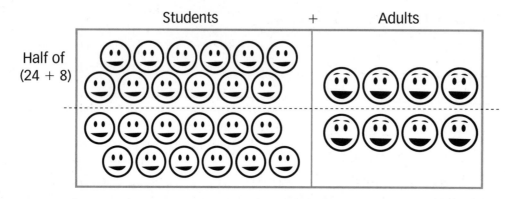

Model It

You can use words to help understand the problem.

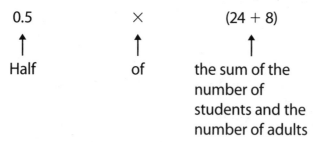

Connect It

Now you will solve the problem from the previous page using the picture and words.

2 Describe one way you could read the expression $0.5 \times (24 + 8)$.

_____

3 How could you use the Picture It on the previous page to evaluate $0.5 \times (24 + 8)$?

_____

_____

4 Evaluate $0.5 \times (24 + 8)$ to find the total cost of the erasers. _____

5 Morgan looks at $0.5 \times (24 + 8)$ and thinks it's easier to find half of 24 and half of 8, and then add those numbers together. Why does her method work?

_____

_____

6 The expression $3 \times$ (number of students + number of adults) represents the cost for another group to go to the dolphin show at the aquarium. Describe how the cost compares to the total number of students and adults.

_____

_____

Try It

Use what you just learned about evaluating expressions to solve these problems. Show your work on a separate sheet of paper.

7 Describe what happens if you multiply a sum by 2.

_____

8 Sara buys a $12 shirt and $26 pants. They are on sale, so she only needs to pay half. Evaluate the expression $\frac{1}{2} \times (12 + 26)$ to find Sara's cost. _____

Read the problem below. Then explore how to write numerical expressions.

Write a numerical expression to represent the following phrase.

15 minus the sum of 6 and 7

Picture It

You can use a picture to help understand the problem.

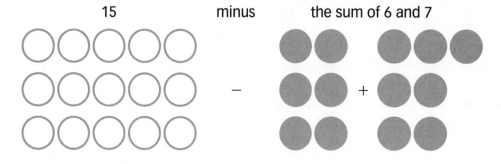

Model It

You can think about what the words mean to help understand the problem.

15 minus	the sum of	6 plus 7
↑	↑	↑
Minus means subtract.	The sum is the result of addition.	Plus means add.

Connect It

Now you will solve the problem from the previous page using the picture and words.

9 In the expression "15 minus the sum of 6 and 7," do you add or subtract first? Why?

_____

10 When you write a numerical expression, how do you show what operation to do first?

_____

_____

11 Write a numerical expression to show "15 minus the sum of 6 plus 7." _____

12 Harper wrote the expression $15 - 6 + 7$ to represent "15 minus the sum of 6 plus 7." Explain to Harper why her expression is incorrect.

_____

_____

13 How you can tell if you need parentheses when you write a numerical expression for a word problem?

_____

_____

Try It

Use what you just learned about writing numerical expressions to solve these problems. Show your work on a separate sheet of paper.

14 Write a numerical expression to represent "2 times the difference of 8 and 1." Then evaluate your expression. _____

15 Write a numerical expression to represent "15 divided by the sum of 1 and 4." Then evaluate your expression.

_____

Study the model below. Then solve problems 16–18.

The student used trial and error to answer the question.

> **Student Model**
>
> Insert parentheses to make the following equation true.
>
> $$15 - 7 - 2 = 10$$
>
> **Look at how you could show your work.**
>
> $$(15 - 7) - 2 = 8 - 2 = 6$$
>
> $$6 \neq 10$$
>
> $$15 - (7 - 2) = 15 - 5 = 10$$
>
> $$10 = 10$$
>
> Solution: $\underline{15 - (7 - 2) = 10}$

Pair/Share

How many different ways can you group the numbers?

How many items did Carol sell altogether?

16 Carol sells bracelets and pairs of earrings at a craft fair. Each item sells for $8. Write and evaluate an expression to show how much money Carol makes if she sells 23 bracelets and 17 pairs of earrings.

Show your work.

Solution: _____

Pair/Share

What other ways could you solve the problem?

17 Write numerical expressions for "the product of 3 and 2, plus 5" and "3 times the sum of 2 and 5." Which expression has a greater value?

Show your work.

Do any of the words represent the result of addition, subtraction, multiplication, or division problem?

Solution: _____

Pair/Share

When do you use parentheses in an expression?

18 Which expression represents "the quotient of 10 and 2, plus 3"? Circle the letter of the correct answer.

A $10 \div (2 + 3)$

B $\dfrac{10}{2 + 3}$

C $(10 \times 2) + 3$

D $\dfrac{10}{2} + 3$

What does the word "quotient" mean?

Jason chose **A** as the correct answer. How did he get that answer?

_____

_____

_____

_____

Pair/Share

Is Jason's answer reasonable?

Solve the problems.

1 Kris ran 3 miles each day for 7 days in a row. One day, she ran an extra $\frac{1}{2}$ mile. Which expression represents how many miles Kris ran altogether?

A $3 + 7 + \frac{1}{2}$

B $3 \times 7 + \frac{1}{2}$

C $3 \times 7 + 3\frac{1}{2}$

D $\left(3 + \frac{1}{2}\right) \times 7$

2 Which expression does NOT represent the statement "divide the difference of 20 and 8 by the sum of 1 and 3"?

A $\frac{20 - 8}{1 + 3}$

B $(20 - 8) \div (1 + 3)$

C $\frac{20}{1 + 3} - \frac{8}{1 + 3}$

D $(20 - 8) \div 1 + 3$

3 Which expression is equal to 8? Circle the letter for all that apply.

A $3 \times 8 \div 4 + 2$

B $3 \times (8 \div 4) + 2$

C $(3 \times 8) \div (4 + 2)$

D $(3 \times 8) \div 4 + 2$

E $3 \times 8 \div (4 + 2)$

4   Adam is 2 years old. His sister Lina is 1 year less than three times his age. Write a numerical expression for Lina's age. _____

5   Several expressions are shown below. Decide if the value of the expression is less than, equal to, or greater than 18. Write each expression in the correct category in the chart.

Less than 18	Equal to 18	Greater than 18

$\frac{1}{5} \times (9 \times 2)$ $(9 \times 2) \times (4 - 3)$ $(9 \times 2) \div 3$ $22 - (9 \times 2)$

$(9 \times 2) + 7$ $4 \times \frac{1}{4} \times (9 \times 2)$ $1 \times (9 \times 2)$ $3 \times (9 \times 2)$

6   Compare the expressions $8 \times 3 + 4$ and $8 \times (3 + 4)$. Explain how to evaluate each expression. Then tell which expression has the greater value.

Show your work.

_____

_____

✓ **Self Check**   *Go back and see what you can check off on the Self Check on page 163.*

Lesson 20   Part 1: Introduction 👥

Analyze Patterns and Relationships

In previous lessons, you learned to identify and extend numerical patterns. Now you will describe the relationship between two patterns. Take a look at this problem.

> Maria is working at the snack stand at a basketball game. Each frozen yogurt costs $3, and each sandwich costs $6. Create a table to show the costs for buying 0, 1, 2, 3, 4, 5, or 6 frozen yogurts. Create another table to show the costs for the same number of sandwiches. How do the costs of frozen yogurts compare to the costs of an equal number of sandwiches?

🔍 Explore It

Use the math you already know to solve the problem.

- What is the cost for buying 1 frozen yogurt? _____

- What do you add to the cost of 1 frozen yogurt to get the cost of 2 frozen yogurts?

  _____

- Complete the table to show the cost for each number of frozen yogurts.

Number of Yogurts	0	1	2	3	4	5	6
Cost ($)							

- What do you add to the cost of 1 sandwich to get the cost of 2 sandwiches?

  _____

- Complete the table to show the cost for each number of sandwiches.

Number of Sandwiches	0	1	2	3	4	5	6
Cost ($)							

- How does the cost of sandwiches compare to the cost of the same number of yogurts?

  _____

  _____

Find Out More

The costs of frozen yogurts and the costs of sandwiches form numerical patterns.

Cost of Frozen Yogurts

+3 +3 +3 +3 +3 +3

0   3   6   9   12   15   18

Cost of Sandwiches

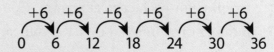

+6 +6 +6 +6 +6 +6

0   6   12   18   24   30   36

You can make a table to help write ordered pairs to see relationships between **corresponding terms** in the two patterns. The first number of each pair is the cost of frozen yogurts, and the second number of the pair is the cost of the same number of sandwiches.

Cost of Yogurts (Add 3)	Cost of Sandwiches (Add 6)	Ordered Pairs
0	0	(0, 0)
3	6	(3, 6)
6	12	(6, 12)
9	18	(9, 18)
12	24	(12, 24)
15	30	(15, 30)
18	36	(18, 36)

There is a relationship between the two numbers of the **ordered pairs**. The second number of each ordered pair is always twice the first number.

Reflect

1 Find the sum of the numbers of each ordered pair. What pattern do you notice?

_____

_____

_____

Read the problem below. Then explore how to identify relationships between two numerical patterns.

> In Level 1 of a game, you get 2 points for each correct answer. In Level 2, you get 6 points for each correct answer. Compare the number of points in Level 2 to the number of points in Level 1 if you correctly answer 0, 1, 2, 3, 4, 5, or 6 questions.

Picture It

You can use a picture to help find each pattern.

Use the number of points for correct answers at each level to find the patterns.

Level 1	Level 2
Each correct answer earns 2 points.	Each correct answer earns 6 points.

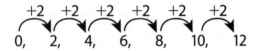

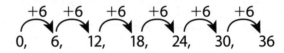

Model It

Use a table to show the number of points you get for correct answers in each level of the game.

Then write ordered pairs where the first number is a term from the first pattern and the second number is the corresponding term from the second pattern.

Points in Level 1	Points in Level 2	Ordered Pairs
0	0	(0, 0)
2	6	(2, 6)
4	12	
6	18	
8	24	
10	30	
12	36	

The total number of points in Level 1 goes up by 2 for each correct answer. The total number of points in Level 2 goes up by 6 for each correct answer.

Connect It

Now you will solve the problem from the previous page by looking at the ordered pairs.

2 Look at Picture It on the previous page. Describe the "rules" for finding the number of points for a correct answer in Level 1 and Level 2.

Level 1 rule: _____

Level 2 rule: _____

3 Complete the table on the previous page.

4 For each ordered pair, how does the second number compare to the first number?

_____

5 Suppose the game has a third level. You get 9 points for each correct answer in that level. Explain how you could figure out how the terms in this pattern compare to the corresponding terms in the pattern for points in Level 2.

_____

_____

_____

_____

Try It

Use what you just learned about comparing two number patterns to solve this problem. Show your work on a separate sheet of paper.

6 School magnets cost $4, and shirts cost $24. Write a pattern for the costs of 0, 1, 2, 3, 4, and 5 magnets and a second pattern for the costs of 0, 1, 2, 3, 4, and 5 shirts. How do the corresponding terms of the two patterns compare?

_____

_____

Read the problem below. Then explore what the graph looks like when you plot corresponding terms of number patterns on a graph.

The scouts have a choice of making a model plane or a model boat. The materials for the plane cost $2, and the materials for the boat cost $4. Write and graph ordered pairs to compare the cost of making one or more planes to the cost of making the same number of boats.

 Picture It

You can use a picture to find the costs of making various numbers of each model.

Each pattern of numbers below shows the cost of making 0, 1, 2, 3, and 4 models.

Planes	Boats

+2 +2 +2 +2
0,   2,   4,   6,   8

+4 +4 +4 +4
0,   4,   8,   12,   16

Model It

You can use a table to help understand the problem.

List the cost for the planes and boats in a table. Then write the corresponding costs as ordered pairs.

Planes (x)	Boats (y)	Ordered Pairs (x, y)
0	0	(0, 0)
2	4	(2, 4)
4	8	(4, 8)
6	12	(6, 12)
8	16	(8, 16)

Connect It

Now you will solve the problem from the previous page by graphing ordered pairs.

7 Explain how to write the ordered pairs from the patterns.

_____

_____

8 Plot the ordered pairs on the graph to the right.
The first number shows the location on the *x*-axis.
The second number shows the location on the *y*-axis.

The point (2, 4) has been plotted for you.

9 How do the coordinates of corresponding terms of the
patterns compare?

_____

_____

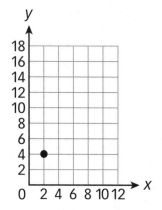

10 Suppose you connect the points. What would the graph look line?

_____

11 What directions would you give to someone to get from one point to the next on the
graph? How do your directions relate to the rules for the patterns?

_____

_____

Try It

**Use what you just learned about comparing two number patterns on a graph to
solve this problem. Show your work on a separate sheet of paper.**

12 Use the rules "add 1" and "add 3" to write and graph ordered pairs made up of
corresponding terms from the two patterns. Start each pattern with 0. Describe
the graph.

_____

_____

Study the model below. Then solve problems 13–15.

The student wrote ordered pairs to identify a relationship between corresponding terms.

Student Model

Look at the following two number patterns.

Pattern 1: 6, 5, 4, 3, 2, 1, 0

Pattern 2: 24, 20, 16, 12, 8, 4, 0

What is the relationship between corresponding terms in the two patterns?

Look at how you could show your work using ordered pairs.

The first coordinate is a term from Pattern 1, the second coordinate is a corresponding term from Pattern 2.
Ordered pairs: (6, 24), (5, 20), (4, 16), (3, 12), (2, 8), (1, 4), (0, 0)

Solution: Each term in Pattern 2 is four times the corresponding term in Pattern 1.

Pair/Share

How are these patterns different from other patterns in this lesson?

How do I generate the sequences?

13 One sequence starts at 0 and has the rule "add 8." Another sequence starts at 0 and has the rule "add 4." Write each sequence of numbers. How do the corresponding terms in the sequences compare?

Show your work.

Pair/Share

Does it matter how many terms you write for each sequence?

Solution: _____

_____

_____

14 Identify the pattern in each column. Then complete the table below. Form ordered pairs for the corresponding terms. Describe the relationship between corresponding terms.

What are the rules for each pattern?

Show your work.

x	y	Ordered Pairs (x, y)
4	1	
8	2	
12	3	

Solution: _____

_____

Pair/Share

Find the difference between the coordinates in each ordered pair. Do you see another pattern?

15 The ordered pairs (2, 12), (3, 18), and (4, 24) were formed by corresponding terms in two sequences. How do the values of the y-coordinates compare to the values of the x-coordinates? Circle the letter of the correct answer.

What rule works for all the points?

A 10 more

B 2 times

C $\frac{1}{6}$ times

D 6 times

Mike chose **C** as the correct answer. How did he get that answer?

_____

_____

_____

Pair/Share

Does Mike's answer make sense?

Solve the problems.

1 What rule could be used to create the pattern 9, 18, 27, 36, 45, 54, . . . ?

A multiply each term by 2 to get the next term

B multiply each term by 9 to get the next term

C add 9 to get the next term

D add 3 to get the next term

2 Look at the patterns below. Choose True or False for each statement.

Pattern 1: 3, 6, 9, 12, 15, 18, . . .

Pattern 2: 18, 36, 54, 72, 90, 108, . . .

A The rule for Pattern 1 is "multiply by 2." ☐ True ☐ False

B The rule for Pattern 2 is "add 18." ☐ True ☐ False

C Each term in Pattern 1 is 6 times the corresponding term in Pattern 2. ☐ True ☐ False

D Each term in Pattern 2 is 3 times the corresponding term in Pattern 1. ☐ True ☐ False

3 Tickets at an outdoor play cost $2 for students and $8 for adults. Jason creates two patterns to compare the costs. He writes ordered pairs in the form (student cost, adult cost) for the corresponding number of tickets. Which ordered pair could be on Jason's list of ordered pairs? Circle the letter for all that apply.

A (8, 2)

B (10, 40)

C (4, 10)

D (10, 16)

E (6, 24)

4 Create two patterns starting with 0 using the rules below. Then describe the relationship between corresponding terms of the two patterns.

Pattern 1: add 3   Pattern 2: add 12

Show your work.

_____

_____

5 Begin at 0 and use the rules "add 2" and "add 5" to complete the table in Part A.

Part A

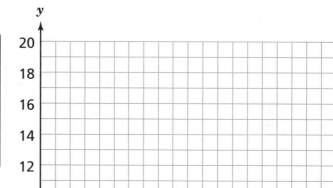

Add 2	Add 5	Ordered Pairs

Part B

Graph the ordered pairs. Describe your graph.

_____

_____

Part C

Describe the relationship between the corresponding terms of the two patterns.

_____

_____

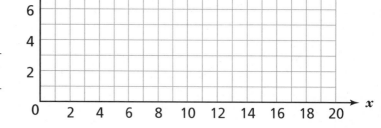 **Self Check** *Go back and see what you can check off on the Self Check on page 163.*

Solve the problems.

1 Casey and 4 friends each bought a $15.00 ticket to the Pro Football Hall of Fame. Casey had a coupon for $10 off the total price of the tickets. Which expression can be used to find the total paid by Casey and his friends?

A $(5 \times 15) - 10$

B $5 \times (15 - 10)$

C $(15 - 10) \times 5$

D $(15 + 10) \times 5$

2 Chloe and Justin made two different number patterns that each started at 0. Chloe wrote terms using the rule "add 18." Justin wrote terms using the rule "add 6." What is the relationship between the two patterns?

A The terms in Chloe's pattern are 3 greater than the corresponding terms in Justin's pattern.

B The terms in Chloe's pattern are 3 less than the corresponding terms in Justin's pattern.

C The terms in Chloe's pattern are 3 times the corresponding terms in Justin's pattern.

D The terms in Chloe's pattern are $\frac{1}{3}$ times the corresponding terms in Justin's pattern.

3 Look at the equations below. Choose *True* or *False* for each equation.

A $15 \div (1 + 4) = 19$

☐ True ☐ False

B $20 - (10 \times 2) = 20$

☐ True ☐ False

C $(5 + 1) \times (5 - 1) = 24$

☐ True ☐ False

D $(12 + 3) \div (10 \div 2) = 3$

☐ True ☐ False

4 Phil created two patterns. For Pattern 1, he started at 0 and used the rule "add 2." The first four terms are 0, 2, 4, and 6. For Pattern 2, he started at 0 and used a rule that added the same number to each term. Each term in Pattern 2 is 10 times the corresponding term in Pattern 1. Complete the table below.

Pattern 1	Pattern 2
0	0
2	
4	
6	

What is the rule for Pattern 2?

The rule for Pattern 2 is _____

5 Staci is learning how to evaluate expressions in math class.

Part A

If Staci correctly evaluates 4 × (6 + 8), what value will she get?

Show your work.

Answer _____

Part B

If the expression is written as 4 × 6 + 8, is the value the same? If not, what is this value?

Show your work.

_____

6 Rick is writing expressions for math class.

Part A

What mathematical expression could Rick write for "subtract 13 from the product of 4 and 7"?

_____

Part B

Compare the expression you wrote in Part A with the expression 5 × (4 × 7 − 13).

_____

_____

Performance Task

Answer the questions and show all your work on separate paper.

Your friend Sophie has asked you to check her math homework for her. She sends you a text message with the expressions she needed to evaluate and the answers she got. Unfortunately, she didn't include any parentheses in her message.

Copy each equation. If the equation is true as written, write a check mark (✓) next to it. If not, insert parentheses to make the equation true.

$6 + 5 \times 3 - 1 = 32$　　　　$12 \div 2 + 4 \times 5 = 10$　　　　$15 - 3 + 4 \times 2 = 20$

$6 + 5 \times 3 - 1 = 16$　　　　$12 \div 2 + 4 \times 5 = 26$　　　　$15 - 3 + 4 \times 2 = 1$

Then write a message to Sophie explaining why she needed to include the parentheses in order for you to check her work.

Reflect on Mathematical Practices

After you complete the task, choose one of the following questions to answer.

1. **Be Precise** How did you decide where to insert the parentheses in each equation?

2. **Use Structure** Consider the expression $6 + 7 \times 5 - 2$. Would you rewrite it as $6 + (7 \times 5) - 2$? Why or why not?

You might say that 52 buckets of sand will fill your backyard sandbox. The clerk at the hardware store where you bought the sand might say the sandbox needs 24 cubic feet of sand. If you would like to cool off in the summer, you could fill your sandbox with water instead of sand. You should know that it will hold about 180 gallons of water. All of these different measurements are ways to talk about the volume of the sandbox.

In this unit, you will find the volume of many different kinds of figures using different units of measurement. You will use what you know about multiplication to find the volume of some figures using a formula.

✓ Self Check

Before starting this unit, check off the skills you know below. As you complete each lesson, see how many more you can check off!

I can:	Before this unit	After this unit
convert from one measurement unit to another, for example: 4 ft = 48 in.	☐	☐
make a line plot of data represented as fractions of measurements	☐	☐
find volume by counting unit cubes	☐	☐
find volume by using a formula	☐	☐
find volume of composite figures	☐	☐

Lesson 21   Part 1: Introduction 👥
Convert Measurement Units

You have worked with measurement units in earlier grades. Now you will convert between different units in the same measurement system.

Is the number of cups in 5 gallons greater than or less than the number of gallons?

1 gallon

1 cup

🔍 Explore It

Use the math you already know to solve the problem.

▪ Circle the greater amount in each row:

  1 gallon   or   1 cup

  2 gallons   or   2 cups

  5 gallons   or   5 cups

▪ If you pour 5 gallons of water into 1-cup containers, would you need more than or fewer than 5 containers? _____

▪ Is the number of cups in 5 gallons greater than or less than the number of gallons?
  _____

Find Out More

You measure for many different reasons. You might measure how long or tall something is, how much liquid something holds, or how much something weighs.

You can choose different units when you measure. Think about your height. You could measure your height in inches or feet. Your height does not change if you are measured in inches versus feet. It is just recorded using different units.

Look at the picture to the right. 1 gallon = 16 cups.

The same amount of liquid could also be measured in quarts. Quarts are smaller than gallons. 1 gallon = 4 quarts. Quarts are larger than cups. 1 quart = 4 cups.

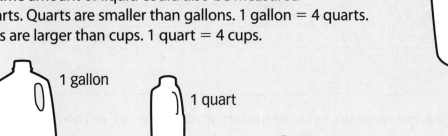

Imagine filling the 1-gallon container using cups or quarts. You would need to fill the quart container 4 times to have enough liquid to fill the gallon container. You would need to fill the cup container 16 times to have enough liquid to fill the gallon container.

The smaller the measurement unit, the more you will need to measure the same amount.

Reflect

1 Describe a real-world object that can be measured and two different units you could use to measure it. Which unit would you need more of to measure the object?

_____

_____

_____

Read the problem below. Then explore different ways to convert measurement units.

How many meters are in 3.5 kilometers?

 Model It

You can use a table to help understand the problem.

The table below shows the relationship between meters and kilometers.

kilometers	1	2	3	4	5	6
meters	1,000	2,000	3,000	4,000	5,000	6,000

Solve It

Use the information from the table to understand how to solve the problem.

The pattern in the table shows that the number of meters is always 1,000 times the number of kilometers.

kilometers	1	2	3	3.5	4	5	6
meters	1,000	2,000	3,000		4,000	5,000	6,000

To find the number of meters in 3.5 kilometers, multiply 3.5 times 1,000.

Connect It

Now you will solve the problem from the previous page using unit conversions.

2 Which is the smaller unit, meters or kilometers? _____ How do you know?

_____

_____

3 What operation do you use to convert from a larger measurement unit to a smaller measurement unit? _____

4 3.5 kilometers = _____ meters.

Write your answer in the table on the previous page.

5 Use what you learned about the relationship between meters and kilometers to complete the table below.

kilometers	0.8	1	1.85	2	2.03	3
meters		1,000		2,000		3,000

6 How many meters are in *x* kilometers? _____

7 There are 3 feet in 1 yard. Explain how you decide whether to multiply or divide by 3 if you need to convert yards to feet. _____

_____

_____

Try It

Use what you just learned about converting measurement units to solve these problems. Show your work on a separate sheet of paper.

8 16 ounces is equivalent to 1 pound. How many ounces are $10\frac{1}{2}$ pounds? _____

9 There are 10 millimeters in 1 centimeter. How many millimeters are in 9.25 centimeters? _____

Read the problem below. Then explore ways to understand how to convert measurement units.

How many quarts are equivalent to 6 cups?

 **Model It**

You can use a table to help understand the problem.

The table below shows the relationship between cups and quarts.

quarts	1	2	3	4	5	6
cups	4	8	12	16	20	24

Solve It

Use the information from the table to understand how to solve the problem.

The pattern in the table shows that there are 4 cups in every quart.

quarts	1		2	3	4	5	6
cups	4	6	8	12	16	20	24

To find the number of quarts equivalent to 6 cups, divide by 4.

🔍 Connect It

Now you will solve the problem from the previous page using unit conversions.

10 Which is a smaller unit, quarts or cups? _____

How do you know? _____

_____

11 What operation do you use to convert from a smaller measurement unit to a larger measurement unit? _____

12 6 cups = _____ quarts. Write your answer in the table on the previous page. Explain your reasoning. _____

_____

13 Use what you learned about the relationship between cups and quarts to complete the table below.

quarts		1		2		3		4
cups	2	4	5	8	9	12	15	16

14 One gallon is equivalent to 8 pints. Describe how to convert from pints to gallons. Explain your reasoning. _____

_____

_____

✏️ Try It

Use what you just learned about converting measurement units to solve these problems. Show your work on a separate sheet of paper.

15 There are 1,000 milliliters in 1 liter. How many liters are in 100 milliliters? _____

16 One yard is equivalent to 3 feet. How many yards are equivalent to 25 feet? _____

Study the model below. Then solve problems 17–19.

Student Model

There are 12 inches in 1 foot. Write 75 inches in feet and inches.

Look at how you could explain your work using conversions.

Feet are larger than inches, so the number of feet will be less than the number of inches. Divide.

There are 12 inches in 1 foot; $75 \div 12 = \frac{75}{12} = 6\frac{3}{12}$.

The whole number, 6, is the number of feet and the fraction $\frac{3}{12}$ is $\frac{3}{12}$ of a foot, or 3 inches.

75 inches = 6 feet, 3 inches

Solution: ___6 feet, 3 inches___

The student used division because inches are smaller than feet!

Pair/Share

How can you check your answer?

How many quarts are in $\frac{1}{2}$ gallon?

Pair/Share

Draw a picture or make a table to support your answer.

---

17 How many quarts are there in $10\frac{1}{2}$ gallons? (4 qt = 1 gal)

Show your work.

Solution: _____

18 One kilogram is equivalent to 1,000 grams. How many kilograms are equivalent to 450 grams?

Show your work.

Will the number of kilograms be greater or less than 450?

Pair/Share
Did you and your partner solve the problem the same way?

Solution: _____

19 There are 1,000 millimeters in 1 meter. How many millimeters are in 118 meters? Circle the letter of the correct answer.

A 0.0118 millimeters

B 0.118 millimeters

C 118,000 millimeters

D 1,180,000 millimeters

Emily chose **B** as the correct answer. How did she get that answer?

_____

_____

_____

_____

Which is a larger unit, millimeters or meters?

Pair/Share
Does Emily's answer make sense?

Solve the problems.

1 How many grams are equivalent to 75 kilograms?

A 0.0075 gram

B 0.075 gram

C 75,000 grams

D 750,000 grams

2 How many yards and feet are equivalent to 10,000 feet?

A 3,333 yards, 0 feet

B 3,333 yards, 1 foot

C 277 yards, 28 feet

D 30,000 yards

3 Write each measurement listed below in the column of the table with an equivalent measure. Some of the measurements may not have an equivalent measure.

$\frac{1}{2}$ quart   4 pints   16 cups $\frac{1}{4}$ gallon   2 pints

1 gallon	1 quart	1 pint

4   Five measurements are shown below. Write one of the measurements in each blank to create two true equations.

300 millimeters   30 meters   3,000 meters   3 kilometers   3,000 centimeters

_____ = _____

_____ = _____

5   How many pints are equivalent to 3 gallons?

Show your work.

Answer _____ pints

6   Complete each conversion below.

Show your work.

3 feet + 7 inches = _____ inches

2 gallons − 5 quarts = _____ quarts

5 pounds − 38 ounces = _____ ounces

60 centimeters + 4 meters = _____ centimeters

2,000 meters + 5,000 meters = _____ kilometers

1 liter − 150 milliliters = _____ milliliters

Units of Length	Units of Capacity	Units of Weight
1 foot = 12 inches	1 quart = 2 pints	1 pound = 16 ounces
1 yard = 3 feet	1 gallon = 4 quarts	
1 mile = 5,280 feet	1 liter = 1,000 milliliters	**Units of Mass**
1 meter = 100 centimeters		1 kilogram = 1,000 grams
1 meter = 1,000 millimeters		

 **Self Check**   *Go back and see what you can check off on the Self Check on page 187.*

Lesson 22   Part 1: Introduction

Solve Word Problems Involving Conversions

In Lesson 21, you converted between different units of measure. In this lesson, you will convert units to solve real-world problems.

Ray has a piece of railing 90 inches long. How long is the railing in yards and inches?

1 yard = 3 feet = 36 inches

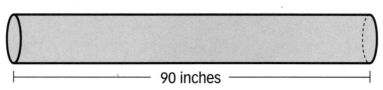

90 inches

🔍 Explore It

Use the math you already know to solve the problem.

▪ The length of the railing is given in what unit? _____

▪ The problems asks to find the length of the railing in what units? _____

▪ Circle the larger unit below.

    yard   inch

▪ To convert yards to inches, what operation do you use? _____

  To convert inches to yards, what operation do you use? _____

▪ 1 yard is equivalent to 3 feet or _____ inches.

▪ Explain how to find 90 inches as yards and inches.

  _____

  _____

🔍 Find Out More

When you convert from one unit of measure to another, you need to know the relationship between the two units.

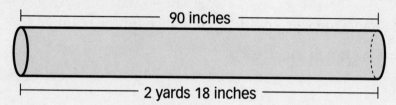

Think about Ray's railing. Instead of yards, he could measure his railing in feet.

To change feet to yards, you need to know that there are 3 feet in 1 yard. Because feet are smaller than yards, you will have more feet than yards.

To change feet to inches, you need to know that there are 12 inches in 1 foot. Because feet are larger than inches, you will have fewer feet than inches.

Look at the relative sizes of 1 yard, 1 foot, and 1 inch.

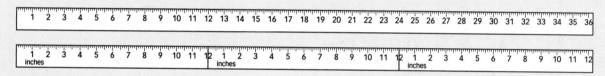

✏️ Reflect

1 Describe how you know whether to multiply or divide when converting one unit of measure to another.

_____

_____

_____

_____

Read the problem below. Then explore different ways to understand how to convert the units to solve the problem.

> Corrina is making punch for a family reunion. Her recipe calls for $2\frac{1}{2}$ cups of lemonade per batch. She wants to make 20 batches of punch for the reunion. How many gallons of lemonade will she need?

Picture It

You can use a picture to understand the relationship between cups and gallons.

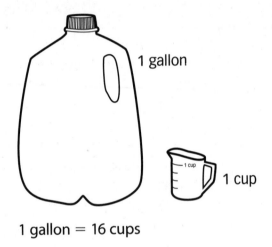

1 gallon

1 cup

1 gallon = 16 cups

Model It

You can write an equation to find the number of cups of lemonade Corrina needs.

Corrina needs to make 20 batches of punch. You need to multiply 20 by the number of cups Corrina needs for 1 batch.

$$20 \times 2\frac{1}{2} = 20 \times \left(2 + \frac{1}{2}\right)$$
$$= 20 \times 2 + 20 \times \frac{1}{2}$$
$$= 40 + 10$$
$$= 50$$

Corrina needs 50 cups of lemonade.

Connect It

Now you will solve the problem from the previous page by converting units.

2 Why do you need to convert units of measure to solve the problem?

_____

_____

_____

3 What operation do you use to convert 50 cups to gallons? Explain.

_____

_____

4 Find the number of gallons of lemonade Corrina will need. Will there be any cups left over?

_____

5 If Corrina could only buy whole gallons of lemonade at the store, how many would she need to buy? _____

Explain your reasoning. _____

_____

_____

6 What if the lemonade was sold in quarts? How could you find the number of quarts Corrina would need? (1 quart = 4 cups) _____

_____

Try It

Use what you just learned about converting units of measure to solve this problem. Show your work on a separate sheet of paper.

7 The pet store salesman told Evan to feed his dog 8 ounces of food per day. The food is sold in pounds. How many pounds does Evan need to buy for 2 weeks of feeding his dog? (16 ounces = 1 pound) _____

Read the problem below. Then explore different ways to understand how to convert the units to solve the problem.

> Heather and Diego measured the worms in their class compost bin. Heather measured a 3.5-centimeter worm, and Diego measured a 28-millimeter worm. Who measured the longer worm?

🔍 Picture It

You can use a picture to help understand the relationship between centimeters and millimeters.

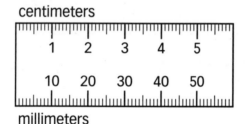

There are 10 millimeters in every centimeter.

🔍 Model It

You can write equations to convert centimeters to millimeters or millimeters to centimeters.

To compare the lengths, both measures need to be in the same unit.

You can convert both measures to either centimeters or millimeters.

To convert centimeters to millimeters:

3.5 cm × 10 = 35 mm

To convert millimeters to centimeters:

28 mm ÷ 10 = 2.8 cm

Connect It

Now you will solve the problem from the previous page by converting units.

8 Why do you need to convert one of the units of measure to solve the problem?

_____

_____

9 Why do you multiply to convert centimeters to millimeters? _____

_____

Why do you divide to convert millimeters to centimeters? _____

_____

10 Who measured the longer worm? How do you know? _____

_____

_____

11 If a third student measured a worm in centimeters, how could you figure out who had the longest worm out of all three students? _____

_____

_____

Try It

Use what you just learned about converting units of measure to solve this problem. Show your work on a separate sheet of paper.

12 A lemur at an animal park weighs 8 pounds, 3 ounces. The zookeeper records the weight of the animals in ounces. What will he write for the weight of the lemur? (1 pound = 16 ounces) _____

Study the model below. Then solve problems 13–15.

Student Model

The student used the relationship between feet and inches to solve the problem.

Pierre is 53 inches tall. How tall is that in feet and inches?

Look at how you could explain your work.

Feet are larger than inches, so there are fewer feet than inches. You need to divide.

There are 12 inches in 1 foot, so divide 53 by 12.

$53 \div 12 = 4$ with a remainder of 5

$= 4$ feet, 5 inches

Solution: ___4 feet, 5 inches___

⬤Pair/Share

What is 53 inches in yards, feet, and inches?

Which is the larger unit, meters or millimeters?

⬤Pair/Share

There are 100 centimeters in 1 meter. How long is the train in centimeters?

13 Venell put together a model train with 25 train cars. Each train car is 80 millimeters long. How many meters long is Venell's model train? (1 meter = 1,000 millimeters)

Show your work.

Solution: _____

14 Orla bought a 1-quart container of buttermilk to make pancakes. Her recipe says to use $\frac{1}{2}$ cup of buttermilk for 3 pancakes. How many pancakes can Orla make? (1 quart = 4 cups)

Show your work.

How many $\frac{1}{2}$ cups are in 1 quart?

Solution: _____

Pair/Share

Make a table to show how much buttermilk is needed for different numbers of pancakes.

15 Bennett is getting in shape for football. He runs 400 yards 3 times each day for 5 days. Which shows the correct way to find the number of miles Bennett will run in 5 days? Circle the letter of the correct answer. (1 mile = 1,760 yards)

A 400 × 3 × 5 × 1,760

B 400 ÷ (3 × 5) ÷ 1,760

C 400 × (3 + 5) ÷ 1,760

D 400 × 3 × 5 ÷ 1,760

Jory chose **A** as the correct answer. How did he get that answer?

_____

_____

_____

Does Bennett run a greater number of miles or a greater number of yards?

Pair/Share

Does Jory's answer make sense?

Solve the problems.

1 A football field is marked every 5 yards. Garrett ran from the first mark to the eleventh mark. Which shows the correct way to find the number of feet Garrett ran?

A $10 \times 5 \div 3$

B $10 \div 5 \div 3$

C $10 \times 5 \times 3$

D 5×3

2 Mr. Wayne's class collected empty soda cans for a recycling project. Each of the 20 students had to collect 40 cans. Each can has a mass of 15 grams. How many kilograms of cans did the class collect to recycle?

1 kilogram = 1,000 grams

A 0.6 kg

B 12 kg

C 12,000 kg

D 12,000,000 kg

3 Susan is stacking boxes on a shelf. Each box is shaped like a rectangular prism and has a length of 2 feet, a width of 15 inches, and a height of 3 inches, as shown below.

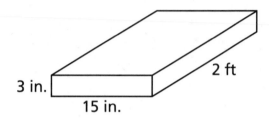

3 in.   15 in.   2 ft

Susan will stack the boxes on top of each other, as shown in this diagram. The space on the shelf is $1\frac{1}{2}$ yards high.

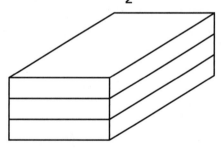

What is greatest number of boxes that Susan can stack on the shelf?

_____ boxes

4   The Russell family is keeping track of the milk they drink each week.

- The first week they drank 2 gallons, 1 quart, and 1 cup of milk.
- The second week they drank 3 gallons of milk.

How many more cups of milk did they drink the second week than the first? _____ cups

1 gallon = 4 quarts = 16 cups

5   Lana's family entered a 5-kilometer race.

1 kilometer = 1,000 meters

Part A

Lana's dad said his average step length is about 1 meter. About how many steps will he need to take to finish the race?

Show your work.

Answer About _____ steps

Part B

Lana's average step length is about 0.5 meter. How many steps will she need to take to finish the race?

Show your work.

Answer About _____ steps

 **Self Check** *Go back and see what you can check off on the Self Check on page 187.*

You have created and used line plots before. Now you will create line plots and use them to answer more complex questions about data. Take a look at this problem.

There are many types of tomatoes of all different sizes. Mrs. May's class weighed several different tomatoes to the nearest $\frac{1}{8}$ pound. The results are shown in the line plot. Use the line plot to describe how much the weights vary.

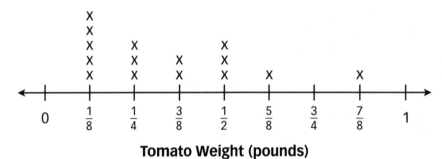

Tomato Weight (pounds)

🔍 Explore It

Use the math you already know to solve the problem.

◼ The greatest number of tomatoes weigh _____ .

◼ Which best describes how the weights are spread out? Circle the best description.

    clustered between   clustered between   spread out
      0 lb and $\frac{1}{2}$ lb $\frac{1}{2}$ and 1 lb   between 0 lb and 1 1b

◼ Are most of the tomatoes on the heavier or lighter end of the scale? _____

◼ Are there any tomatoes whose weight is very different from the rest?

    If so, what does it weigh? _____

◼ What is the difference between the heaviest and lightest tomato? _____

◼ How many times the weight of the lightest tomato is the heaviest tomato? _____

Find Out More

Plotting data on a line plot helps you get a "picture" of what it looks like and how it is spread out. The taller bars mean more data points at that value since each X represents one piece of data.

You can use the tomato-weight line plot to talk about the distribution of tomato weights. **Distribution** is how spread out or how clustered the pieces of data are.

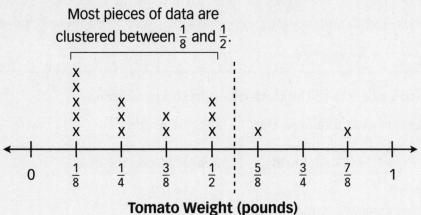

Tomato Weight (pounds)

You can also use operations with the pieces of data to describe the data altogether. For example:

- Subtract $\frac{7}{8} - \frac{1}{8}$ to find the difference between the heaviest and lightest tomato. This shows how much the weights vary.

- Divide or multiply to find that the heaviest tomato is 7 times as heavy as the lightest tomato: $\frac{1}{8} \times 7 = \frac{7}{8}$. This compares pieces of data.

Reflect

1 Describe a real-world set of data that you could show on a line plot.

_____

_____

_____

Read the problem below. Then explore different ways to understand how to create a line plot.

Kiera bought a bag of stickers to decorate her scrapbook pages. She sorted and counted the stickers by width. 18 stickers are $\frac{1}{4}$ inch wide, 11 stickers are $\frac{1}{2}$ inch wide, and 14 stickers are $\frac{1}{8}$ inch wide. Kiera wants to see the distribution of the widths so she can plan how to use them. Make a line plot of the data.

 **Model It**

You can use a table to understand the data given in the problem.

List the number of stickers in a table from least to greatest width.

Sticker Width (inch)	Number of Stickers
$\frac{1}{8}$	14
$\frac{1}{4}$	18
$\frac{1}{2}$	11

Model It

Use the table to list what you know and plan how to make the line plot.

- The fractions are in halves, fourths, and eighths.
- The least fraction is $\frac{1}{8}$. The greatest fraction is $\frac{1}{2}$.
- Label the line plot in eighths: $0, \frac{1}{8}, \frac{1}{4}, \frac{3}{8}, \frac{1}{2}$.
- The least number of stickers is 11.
- The greatest number of stickers is 18.

Connect It

Now you will make the line plot for the problem on the previous page.

2 What scale is used for the line plot? Explain.

_____

_____

3 How many Xs will you draw at each width?

$\frac{1}{8}$ in. _____ $\frac{1}{4}$ in. _____ $\frac{3}{8}$ in. _____ $\frac{1}{2}$ in. _____

4 Use the number line to the right to make a line plot of the sticker widths.

5 Based on how the data are grouped, what is one conclusion you can make about Kiera's stickers?

_____

_____

6 How do you use a line plot to group
measurement data? Why? _____

_____

_____

_____

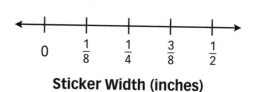

Sticker Width (inches)

Try It

Use what you just learned about creating line plots to solve this problem.

7 At a health fair, Shawn recorded the number of cups of sugar per gallon for several different sports drinks and sodas. Make a line plot of the data.

$$1\frac{5}{8}, 3\frac{1}{4}, 1\frac{3}{4}, 2\frac{7}{8}, 1\frac{3}{4}, 3\frac{1}{4}, 1\frac{5}{8}, 2\frac{3}{8}, 1, 1\frac{3}{4}$$

Read the problem below. Then explore different ways to understand how to solve the problem using the data from the line plot.

> Look at the line plot of sticker widths that you made on the previous page. Kiera wants to make a 5-inch wide row of stickers under a photo. She wants to use the same stickers for the whole row. How many of which width of sticker can she use?

Picture It

You can use a picture to help understand the data in the problem.

Kiera has 14 stickers that are $\frac{1}{8}$-inch wide:

☐ = $\frac{1}{8}$ inch

1" $1\frac{6}{8}$ "

Kiera has 18 stickers that are $\frac{1}{4}$-inch wide:

😊 = $\frac{1}{4}$ inch

1"   2"   3"   4" $4\frac{2}{4}$ "

Kiera has 11 stickers that are $\frac{1}{2}$-inch wide:

⭐ = $\frac{1}{2}$ inch

1"   2"   3"   4"   5" $5\frac{1}{2}$ "

Model It

You can use a model to help understand the data in the problem.

Line up the number of each width of sticker on a ruler.

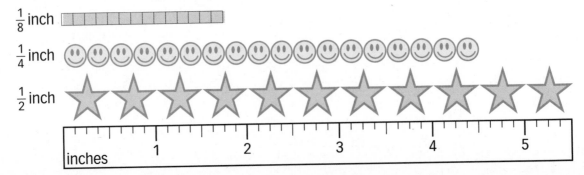

$\frac{1}{8}$ inch

$\frac{1}{4}$ inch

$\frac{1}{2}$ inch

inches   1   2   3   4   5

Connect It

Now you will solve the problem from the previous page using the line plot.

8 How wide is the row Kiera can make with the $\frac{1}{8}$-inch stickers? _____

9 Can she make a 5-inch row with the $\frac{1}{4}$-inch stickers? Show why. _____

10 Can she make a 5-inch row with the $\frac{1}{2}$-inch stickers? Show why. _____

11 Which sticker width does Kiera need to use to make a 5-inch row? _____

How many of these stickers does she need? Explain.

_____

12 How did the line plot help you to answer the question? _____

_____

_____

_____

13 Give an example of another question that can be answered using the line plot. Include the answer. _____

_____

_____

Try It

Use what you just learned about using data in line plots to solve these problems. Show your work on a separate sheet of paper.

Look at the line plot you made about the amount of sugar in different drinks on page 211.

14 How many times the sugar in the drink with the least sugar is in the drink with the most sugar? _____

15 If you combine all of the sugar in the three drinks with the most sugar, and then you redistribute it equally among those 3 drinks, how many cups of sugar would there be per gallon? _____

Study the model below. Then solve problems 16–18.

Student Model

Mel recorded the number of hamburgers of different weights that she made for a cookout. The line plot shows her data.

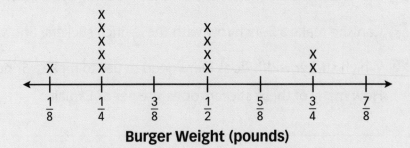

Burger Weight (pounds)

How many pounds of meat did she use to make all the burgers?

Look at how you could use the data in the line plot.

One $\frac{1}{8}$-lb burger: $\frac{1}{8}$ 　　　　　　Total: $\frac{1}{8} + 1\frac{1}{4} + 2 + 1\frac{1}{2} = 4\frac{7}{8}$

Five $\frac{1}{4}$-lb burgers: $5 \times \frac{1}{4} = 1\frac{1}{4}$

Four $\frac{1}{2}$-lb burgers: $4 \times \frac{1}{2} = 2$

Two $\frac{3}{4}$-lb burgers: $2 \times \frac{3}{4} = 1\frac{1}{2}$

Solution: _____$4\frac{7}{8}$ pounds_____

🗨 Pair/Share

Check the student's answer using addition instead of multiplication.

A $\frac{1}{2}$-pound burger could be two $\frac{1}{4}$-pound patties put together.

16 Look at Mel's hamburger line plot above.

One friend at the cookout asks for a triple quarter-pound burger. At what point on the number line could that burger be represented?

Show your work.

🗨 Pair/Share

Draw a picture to show how you figured out what a triple quarter-pound burger is.

Solution: _____

17 A veterinarian's scale weighs animals to the nearest one eighth of a pound. The list below shows the weights, in pounds, of the last 14 dogs that the veterinarian saw.

$15\frac{1}{8}$, 19, $17\frac{1}{2}$, $15\frac{1}{8}$, $16\frac{1}{4}$, $17\frac{1}{2}$, $17\frac{1}{2}$, $18\frac{1}{4}$, $16\frac{5}{8}$, $14\frac{1}{4}$, 19, $17\frac{3}{8}$, $17\frac{1}{8}$, 18

Create a line plot to show the data.

Solution:

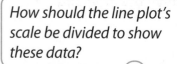

How should the line plot's scale be divided to show these data?

💬 **Pair/Share**

How is your line plot the same as your partner's? How is it different?

18 Look at your line plot for problem 17. Which statement about the data is true? Circle the letter of the correct answer.

A The heaviest dog weighed about 5 times as much as the lightest dog.

B Most of the dogs weighed more than 17 pounds.

C All of the dogs weighed between 15 and 19 pounds.

D At most, only 2 dogs weighed the same amount.

Michelle chose **A** as the correct answer. How did she get that answer?

_____

_____

_____

_____

Read each statement carefully and check it against the data to see if it is true.

💬 **Pair/Share**

Does Michelle's answer make sense?

Solve the problems.

1   Juan drives a race car. The race tracks vary in length. To prepare for the racing season, he recorded the lengths, in miles, of the tracks below. Juan would like to see the distribution of track sizes. Which line plot shows the track data?

$$\frac{1}{4}, \frac{1}{2}, \frac{3}{8}, \frac{1}{2}, \frac{1}{4}, \frac{1}{2}, 1, 1\frac{1}{4}, \frac{3}{4}, \frac{1}{2}, \frac{7}{8}, \frac{1}{2}, \frac{3}{4}$$

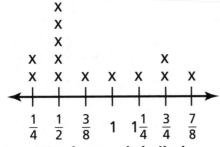

Track Length (miles)

A

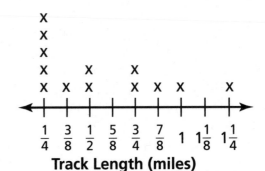

Track Length (miles)

C

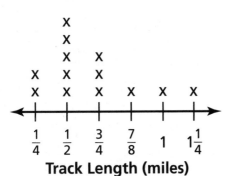

Track Length (miles)

B

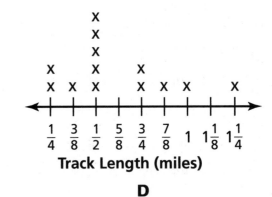

Track Length (miles)

D

2   Look at the data in problem 1. Choose *True* or *False* for each statement.

A   Most of the tracks are more than 1 mile long.   ☐ True   ☐ False

B   The most common track length is $\frac{1}{4}$ mile.   ☐ True   ☐ False

C   None of the tracks are $\frac{5}{8}$ mile long.   ☐ True   ☐ False

D   The longest track is 5 times as long as the shortest track.   ☐ True   ☐ False

3 Look at the data in problem 1. What is the total length of all the tracks that are longer than $\frac{5}{8}$ mile? _____ miles

4 Sara owns Sara's Hardware. She made the line plot below to compare the amounts of fuel that several types of yard trimmers hold.

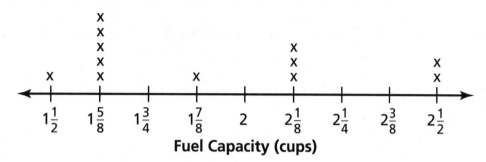

Fuel Capacity (cups)

Part A

What is the capacity of most of the trimmers Sara sells?

Answer _____ cups

Part B

Sara needs to fill the fuel tank of one of each type of trimmer for a demonstration. How much fuel does she need?

Show your work.

Answer _____ cups

 **Self Check** *Go back and see what you can check off on the Self Check on page 187.*

Lesson 24   Part 1: Introduction

Understand Volume

What does volume measure?

Volume tells how many cubes of a particular size it takes to fill a solid figure.

A cube with a side length of 1 unit is called a unit cube. It has one **cubic unit** of volume.

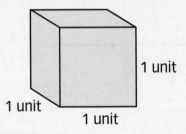

1 unit

1 unit

1 unit

The units used to measure volume are based on the units used to measure length. For example, if the side length of the cube pictured above were 1 inch, then the volume of the cube would be 1 cubic inch.

🔍 Think   How is volume different from area?

Area is the number of *square units* needed to *cover* a *plane* figure. Volume is the number of *cubic units* needed to *fill* a *solid* figure.

Circle the figures below that have volume.

To measure the area of a plane figure, you measure in two dimensions: length and width. You can measure the area of a plane figure by covering it with unit squares.

To measure the space inside a solid figure, or three-dimensional figure, you have to measure in three directions: length, width, and height. You can measure the volume of a solid figure by packing it with unit cubes.

1 unit

1 unit

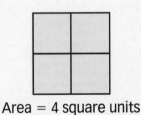

Area = 4 square units

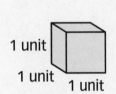

1 unit

1 unit

1 unit

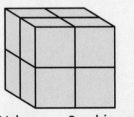

Volume = 8 cubic units

🔍 Think When might you need to measure volume?

Suppose you need to buy a storage box to hold all of your blocks. How would you decide which storage box to buy?

One way to compare the size of containers is by volume.

If you know the volume of each block and the total volume of the storage box, then you could make sure you buy a box big enough to hold all of the blocks.

I need to count how many blocks are in the whole box, but I can't see all of the blocks. I can see that there are 16 blocks in 1 layer and that there are 4 of the same-size layers. 16 + 16 + 16 + 16 = 64

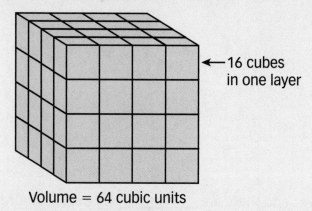

← 16 cubes in one layer

Volume = 64 cubic units

✏️ Reflect

1 Explain the difference between 9 square units and 9 cubic units.

_____

_____

_____

_____

Explore It

You can use unit cubes to build or fill a solid figure. The volume of the figure is the number of unit cubes needed to build or fill it.

2 The measure of each side length of a unit cube is _____.

3 The volume of each unit cube is _____.

Alexander stacked unit cubes to build the figure below. Use the figure to answer problems 4 and 5.

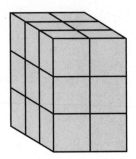

4 There are _____ cubes in 1 layer, and there are _____ layers. The figure has _____ blocks.

5 The volume of the figure is _____ cubic units.

Now try these two problems. Use the figures to answer problems 6 and 7.

A   B

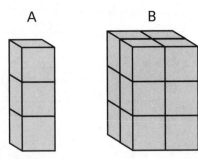

The volume of each block is 1 cubic unit.

6 What is the volume of figure A? _____

7 How many of figure A does it take to fill or build figure B? _____

What is the volume of figure B? _____

🗨 Talk About It

Solve the problems below as a group.

8 Why do you use cubic units and not square units to find the volume of solid figures?

_____

_____

9 Candace places blocks measuring 1 cubic unit into her jewelry box, as shown to the right.

How many blocks does it take to fill the jewelry box? _____

What is the volume of Candace's jewelry box? _____

1 cubic unit

10 Candace has another jewelry box a little like this one. It holds 1 more layer of blocks. What is the volume of this box?

_____

_____

✏ Try It Another Way

Work with your group to show the connection between volume, the number of layers, and the number of unit cubes in each layer.

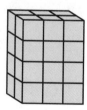

11 How many unit cubes are in each layer? _____

How many of these same layers are in the figure? _____

12 Explain how you can use multiplication to find the volume of the figure.

_____

_____

Connect It

Talk through these problems as a class, then write your answers below.

13 Infer: Eli said, "The volume of this box is 18 cubic units."

Explain how Eli found the volume of the box. _____

_____

_____

14 Explain: Zoe says that a box that is 1 unit wide, 2 units long, and 3 units tall has a greater volume than a box that is 2 units wide, 3 units long, and 1 unit tall. Is she correct? Explain your answer.

_____

_____

_____

_____

15 Compare: Which box has less volume? Explain your answer.

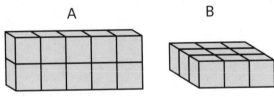

A   B

Each block is 1 cubic unit.

_____

_____

Put It Together

16 Use what you have learned to complete this task.

Niles used 16 blocks, each measuring 1 cubic unit, to build a rectangular prism.

A   Draw or build a model to represent the situation.

B   Look at your model. Describe the number of layers and the number of cubes in each layer. Then describe a different rectangular prism that has a volume of 16 cubic units.

_____

_____

_____

_____

_____

Lesson 25   Part 1: Introduction

Find Volume Using Unit Cubes

In Lesson 24, you learned that you can fill a solid figure with unit cubes to find its volume. Now take a look at this problem.

Carl filled the box shown below with unit cubes to find its volume.

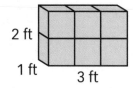

2 ft

1 ft   3 ft

What is the volume of the box?

🔍 Explore It

Use the math you already know to solve the problem.

▪ How many cubes are in the bottom layer of the box? _____

▪ How many cubes are in each layer? _____

▪ How many layers of cubes are in the box? _____

▪ Should Carl use square units or cubic units to find the volume of the box? Explain.

_____

_____

▪ Describe how Carl can find the volume, including what unit he needs to use.

_____

_____

_____

Find Out More

The box on the previous page is a rectangular prism. The volume of any rectangular prism is the amount of space inside it.

To measure volume, you need a unit with three dimensions, like a cube. Volume is always measured in cubic units.

The units used to measure volume are based on the units used to measure length. For example, the box has side lengths measured in feet, so its volume is measured in cubic feet. Each cube in the box is 1 foot long, 1 foot wide, and 1 foot tall.

1 ft
1 ft   1 ft

One way to find the volume of the box is to count how many cubes fill the box. There are a total of 6 cubes in the box. So, the volume of the box is 6 cubic feet.

Here are some other units for measuring volume:

Units of Volume	cubic inch	cubic centimeter
Unit Cube	1 in. 1 in. 1 in.	1 cm 1 cm 1 cm

Reflect

1 Suppose Carl's box was 4 feet tall instead of 2 feet. What would be its volume? Explain your reasoning.

_____

_____

_____

Read the problem below. Then explore different ways to find the volume of a rectangular prism.

Abigail built this rectangular prism from cardboard.

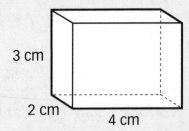

3 cm

2 cm

4 cm

What is the volume of the prism?

 **Model It**

You can find the volume of the prism by filling it with cubes and counting.

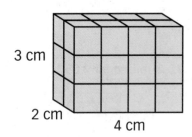

3 cm

2 cm

4 cm

24 cubes fill the rectangular prism.

 **Model It**

You can also find the volume by counting the cubes in each layer, and then adding the number of cubes in each layer.

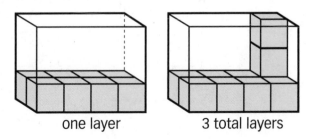

one layer   3 total layers

There are 8 cubes in each layer and 3 layers in all.

8 cubes + 8 cube + 8 cube = 24 cubes in all

Connect It

Now you will solve the problem from the previous page by multiplying.

2 Look at the models. How could you find the number of cubes in one layer without having to count? _____

_____

3 Once you know how many cubes are in one layer, what else do you need to know to find the volume? _____

4 Since there are 8 cubes in each layer, and you know there are 3 layers, what multiplication expression can you write to find the volume of the prism? _____

5 What is the volume of Abigail's rectangular prism? _____

6 Explain how you can use multiplication to find the volume of any rectangular prism.

_____

_____

_____

Try It

Use what you just learned about ways to find the volume of a rectangular prism to solve these problems. Show your work on a separate sheet of paper.

7 What is the volume of this rectangular prism? _____

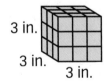

3 in.

3 in.

3 in.

8 Mr. Wong filled the box below with 1-foot cubes to find its volume.

2 ft

1 ft

2 ft

What is the volume of Mr. Wong's box? _____

Study the model below Then solve problems 9–11.

The student started by finding the number of cubes in the bottom layer.

Pedro knows that his storage box has a volume of 36 cubic feet. He knows that the box is 4 feet long and 3 feet wide. How tall is the box?

Look at how you could show your work using a drawing and multiplication facts.

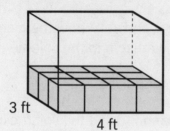

3 ft

4 ft

3 × 4 = 12

12 × ☐ = 36

☐ = 36 ÷ 12

☐ = 3

Solution: __3 feet__

Pair/Share
Could you solve this problem another way?

How many layers of cubes will there be?

9 A box measures 6 centimeters long, 2 centimeters wide, and 4 centimeters tall. What is the volume of the box?

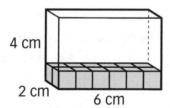

4 cm

2 cm

6 cm

Show your work.

Pair/Share
Can you use multiplication to solve this problem?

Solution: _____

10 Kamala filled the box below with cubes to find its volume.

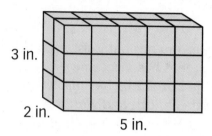

3 in.

2 in.

5 in.

What is the volume of Kamala's box?

Show your work.

Solution: _____

How many cubes are there in each layer?

Pair/Share

How did you decide which method to use to solve the problem?

11 What is the volume of this rectangular prism?

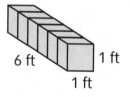

6 ft   1 ft

1 ft

A   6 square feet

B   6 cubic feet

C   8 square feet

D   8 cubic feet

Nam chose **D** as the correct answer. How did he get that answer?

_____

_____

_____

Should I add or multiply to find the answer?

Pair/Share

Does Nam's answer make sense?

Solve the problems.

1   How many cubes are in the bottom layer of this prism?

A   3

B   6

C   12

D   24

2   Which expression can be used to find the volume of this rectangular prism? Circle the letter for all that apply.

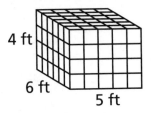

4 ft
6 ft
5 ft

A 30×4

B $(5 + 6) \times 4$

C $30 + 30 + 30 + 30$

D $5 + 6 + 4$

E $30 + 4$

3   Flora is packing her baby sister's blocks into a box that has a volume of 24 cubic inches. The box is 2 inches tall. What could be the length and width of the box? Select *Yes* or *No* for each length and width.

A   11 inches long, 11 inches wide

☐ Yes   ☐ No

B   4 inches long, 3 inches wide

☐ Yes   ☐ No

C   2 inches long, 10 inches wide

☐ Yes   ☐ No

D   6 inches long, 2 inches wide

☐ Yes   ☐ No

E   1 inch long, 12 inches wide

☐ Yes   ☐ No

4   Which rectangular prism has the greater volume, figure A or figure B?

Show your work.

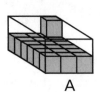

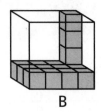

A   B

Answer _____ has the greater volume.

5   Mato built this prism that is 5 centimeters by 2 centimeters by 4 centimeters.

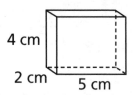

4 cm

2 cm   5 cm

Part A

Draw a different prism with the same volume as Mato's prism.

Part B

Explain how you know the volume of your prism is the same as Mato's prism.

_____

_____

_____

✓ **Self Check** *Go back and see what you can check off on the Self Check on page 187.*

Lesson 26   Part 1: Introduction 👥

Find Volume Using Formulas

In previous lessons, you learned how to find volume by counting cubes. In this lesson, you will learn how to find volume using formulas. Take a look at this problem.

> Becky uses 1-inch cubes to create a model for a small paper gift bag she is making. Her model is a rectangular prism. What is the volume of Becky's model?
>
>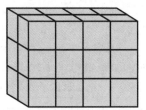

🔍 Explore It

Use the math you already know to solve the problem.

▪ The model has a length of _____ inches and a width of _____ inches.

▪ How many cubes are in the bottom layer? _____

How can you find the number of cubes in the bottom layer without counting?

_____

▪ How many layers does the prism have? _____

▪ How many cubes are in Becky's model? _____

▪ Explain how you can find the volume of Becky's model without counting each cube.

_____

_____

_____

Find Out More

Here is a picture of Becky's gift bag next to her model.

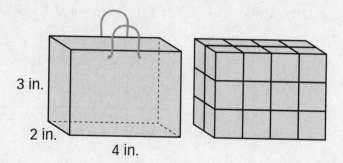

3 in.

2 in.

4 in.

Notice that the base of the bag is a rectangle 4 inches long and 2 inches wide. The area of the base is 8 square inches. The height of the bag is 3 inches.

Look at the model. There are 8 cubes in every layer. There are 3 layers of blocks.

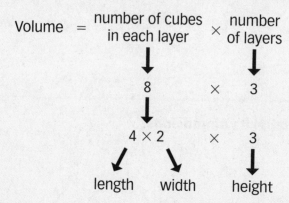

Volume = number of cubes in each layer × number of layers

8 × 3

4 × 2 × 3

length   width   height

Volume = length × width × height

Reflect

1 The area of the base of the gift bag is the product of the length and width. How can you use the area of the base of the gift bag model to find its volume?

_____

_____

_____

Read the problem below. Then explore different ways to find the volume of a rectangular prism.

Gareth has a rectangular pencil cup at his desk. The cup is 3 inches long, 2 inches wide, and 5 inches tall. What is the volume of the pencil cup?

🔍 Picture It

You can picture the problem as a rectangular prism made up of 1-inch cubes.

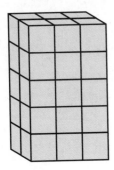

🔍 Model It

You can draw a model of the prism and label its dimensions.

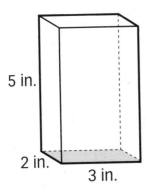

5 in.

2 in.

3 in.

Connect It

Now you will solve the problem from the previous page using the picture and model of the pencil cup.

2 Describe how you can find the volume of the pencil cup using the picture.

_____

_____

_____

3 Explain how the area of the base of the prism in Model It relates to the prism in Picture It. _____

_____

4 Explain how you can find the volume of the pencil cup using the model.

_____

_____

_____

5 Write two different equations to show how you can find the volume of the pencil cup.

_____

6 Explain how you can use the dimensions of a rectangular prism to find its volume.

_____

_____

Try It

Use what you just learned about finding volume to solve these problems. Show your work on a separate sheet of paper.

7 What is the volume of a jewelry box with a length of 8 centimeters, a width of 5 centimeters, and a height of 4 centimeters? _____

8 How much space is taken up by a book that is 12 inches long, 10 inches wide, and 1 inch thick? _____

Study the solution below. Then solve problems 9–11.

Student Model

The student wrote an equation using the formula for volume. The height is the unknown.

Coen is digging a hole for a tomato plant. The plant is in 45 cubic inches of soil in a container with a 3-inch wide and 3-inch long base. How deep does Coen need to dig the hole if the top of the plant's soil should be level with the ground?

Look at how you could use a formula to solve the problem.

$$Volume = l \times w \times h$$

$$45 = 3 \times 3 \times h$$
$$45 = 9 \times h$$
$$45 \div 9 = h$$

$$h = 5$$

Solution: ___5 inches___

🗨 **Pair/Share**

Did you and your partner solve the problem the same way?

9 Evie uses 20 square inches of cardboard for the base of a box. The box has a height of 6 inches. What is the volume of the box?

Show your work.

What does 20 square inches represent?

🗨 **Pair/Share**

What are some possible dimensions of the base of the box?

Solution: _____

10 The rectangular prism shown below has a volume of 42 cubic meters. What is the length of the prism?

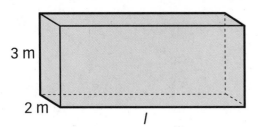

3 m

2 m

l

Show your work.

Solution: _____

11 A cube is a rectangular prism whose edge lengths are congruent. What is the volume of a cube with an edge length of 2 feet? Circle the letter of the correct answer.

A 4 cubic feet

B 6 cubic feet

C 8 cubic feet

D 12 cubic feet

Danny chose **B** as the correct answer. How did he get that answer?

_____

_____

_____

Solve the problems.

1 A rectangular prism has a square base with side lengths of 5 centimeters and a height of 7 centimeters. What is the volume of the prism?

A 35 cubic centimeters

B 140 cubic centimeters

C 175 cubic centimeters

D 245 cubic centimeters

2 A rectangular prism has a volume of 100 cubic meters. One of the dimensions is 5 meters. Which could be the other two dimensions of the prism? Circle the letter for all that apply.

A 1 meter, 20 meters

B 5 meters, 10 meters

C 10 meters, 10 meters

D 4 meters, 5 meters

E 20 meters, 20 meters

3 Henry pours 960 cubic inches of sand into the fish tank shown. Using the number line as a guide, shade the bottom of the tank to show the height of the sand.

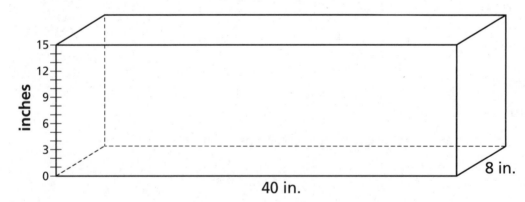

4   A cardboard box has a volume of 60 cubic feet. Give four sets of measurements that could be the dimensions of the box.

Show your work.

☐ feet × ☐ feet × ☐ feet

☐ feet × ☐ feet × ☐ feet

☐ feet × ☐ feet × ☐ feet

☐ feet × ☐ feet × ☐ feet

5   A fish tank that is 12 inches long, 6 inches wide, and 8 inches high has enough room to safely hold 3 guppies. The number of guppies that a fish tank can safely hold depends on its volume. How many guppies can a fish tank that is 24 inches long, 12 inches wide, and 16 inches high safely hold?

Show your work.

Answer _____ guppies

✓ **Self Check**   *Go back and see what you can check off on the Self Check on page 187.*

Find Volume of Composite Figures

You learned how to use a formula to find the volume of a rectangular prism. In this lesson, you will add to find the volume of a solid figure made up of more than one rectangular prism. Take a look at this problem.

What is the volume of this L-shaped solid figure?

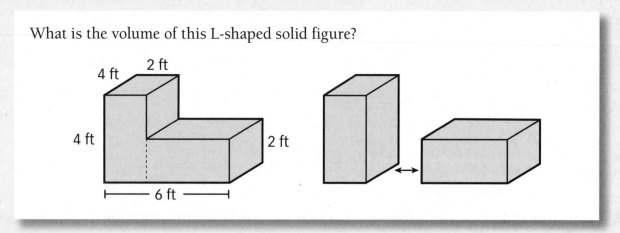

🔍 Explore It

Use the math you already know to solve the problem.

- Look at the dashed segment in the figure. Imagine slicing the solid figure along it to make two rectangular prisms.

  What would be the dimensions of the prism on the left? _____

  What would be the dimensions of the prism on the right? _____

- How could you find the volume of each prism? _____

- What is the volume of each prism? _____

- How could you find the volume of the figure made up of these two prisms?

  _____

- What is the volume of the original solid figure? _____

Find Out More

Rectangles can be combined in different ways to create different two-dimensional shapes. You can find the area of these shapes by breaking them apart into the rectangles that make them up. There may be more than one way to break apart the figures.

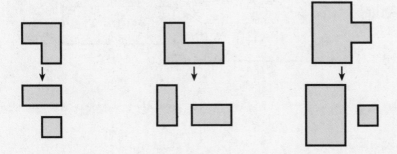

Rectangular prisms can be combined in different ways to make solid figures. You can find the volume of these solid figures by breaking them apart into the prisms that make them up. There may be more than one way to break apart the solid figures.

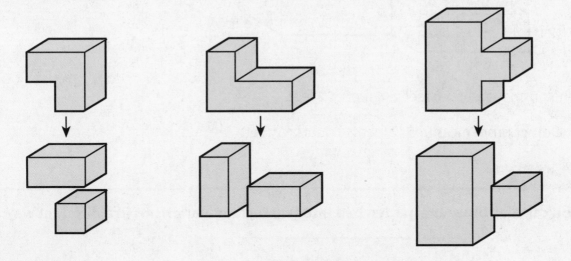

Reflect

1 Circle one of the solids above. Explain how you would find its volume.

_____

_____

_____

Read the problem. Then explore different ways to break apart a solid figure into rectangular prisms to find its volume.

Bethany is making a garden bed. The diagram shows its measurements. If she fills the bed to the top with soil, how many cubic feet of soil will Bethany need?

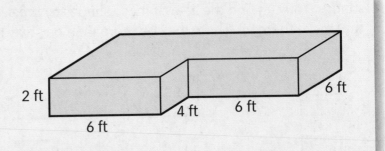

Model It

You can break the garden bed into two rectangular prisms this way.

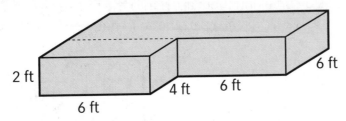

One prism measures 6 feet × 4 feet × 2 feet.

The other prism measures 12 feet × 6 feet × 2 feet.

Model It

You can also break the garden bed into two rectangular prisms in a different way.

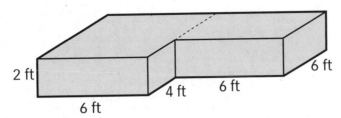

One prism measures 6 feet × 10 feet × 2 feet.

The other prism measures 6 feet × 6 feet × 2 feet.

Connect It

Now you will solve the problem from the previous page using a formula.

2 Look at the first model. How can you find the volume of each prism?

_____

3 How can you find the volume of the entire garden bed?

_____

4 What is the volume of the entire garden bed? Show your work. _____

5 Now look at the second model. Show how to find the volume of the garden bed if you break it apart this way.

6 Does it matter how you break apart a solid figure to find its volume? Use this problem to explain your reasoning. _____

_____

Try It

Use what you just learned about breaking apart solid figures to solve these problems. Show your work on a separate sheet of paper.

7 The Recreation Center has an L-shaped pool. One part of the pool is 8 meters by 6 meters. The other part is 12 meters by 6 meters. The whole pool is 4 meters deep. What is the volume of the entire pool? _____

8 What is the volume of this solid figure? _____

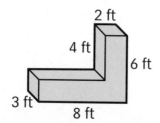

Study the model below. Then solve problems 9–11.

The student drew a dashed segment to show where the break is.

Student Model

Adima filled this tiered flowerpot to the top with potting soil. What is the total volume of the flowerpot?

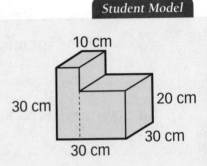

Look at how you could break apart the figure into two rectangular prisms.

$20 \times 30 \times 20 = 12,000$
$10 \times 30 \times 30 = 9,000$

$12,000 + 9,000 = 21,000$

Solution: **21,000 cubic centimeters**

⬤Pair/Share

Could you break apart the solid figure in a different way?

Would it help to draw a diagram to represent the problem?

9 Tia made a 2-layer cake. Each layer is a 2-inch high rectangular prism. The base of the bottom layer is 100 square inches. The base of the top layer is 64 square inches. What is the total volume of the cake?

Show your work.

⬤Pair/Share

Can you solve the problem in a different way?

Solution: _____

10 The diagram shows the shape of a cement walkway. What is the total volume of cement needed to make the walkway?

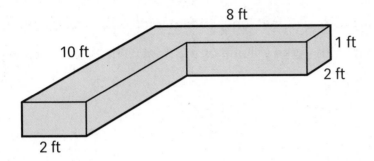

8 ft

10 ft

1 ft

2 ft

2 ft

Show your work.

Solution: _____

How will I find the missing measurements?

⬤Pair/Share

How did you and your partner decide how to break apart the solid figure?

11 Workers are replacing some square pipes at a gas station. The sides of the pipes are 2 inches long. One worker joins a pipe 48 inches long to one that is twice its length. The pipes do not overlap each other. What is the total volume of the two pipes joined together?

A 96 cubic inches

B 144 cubic inches

C 288 cubic inches

D 576 cubic inches

Kali chose **B** as the correct answer. How did she get that answer?

_____

_____

_____

What is the total length of the pipe?

⬤Pair/Share

Does Kali's answer make sense?

Solve the problems.

1   A pool shaped like a rectangular prism is 40 feet long, 20 feet wide, and 4 feet deep. Attached to the side of the pool is a hot tub with $\frac{1}{4}$ the volume of the pool. What is the total volume of the pool and hot tub?

    A   800 cubic feet

    B   1,000 cubic feet

    C   3,200 cubic feet

    D   4,000 cubic feet

2   The diagram shows the measurements of a mold used to make sandcastles. Which expression can be used to find the volume of the mold? Circle the letter for all that apply.

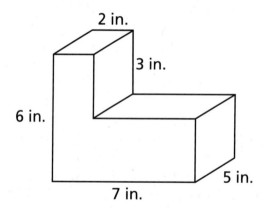

    A $(2 \times 5 \times 3) + (5 \times 5 \times 3)$

    B $(2 \times 5 \times 3) + (7 \times 5 \times 3)$

    C $(2 \times 5 \times 6) + (5 \times 5 \times 3)$

    D $(2 \times 5 \times 6) + (7 \times 5 \times 3)$

    E $(2 \times 5 \times 3) + (7 \times 5 \times 6)$

3 This diagram shows the dimensions of two identical rectangular prisms joined together.

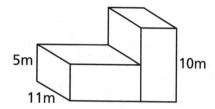

5m

10m

11m

What is the combined volume of these prisms? _____ cubic meters

4 Rami designed a small pond with a waterfall for a restaurant. The diagram shows the measurements of the pond. How many cubic feet of water are needed to fill the pond?

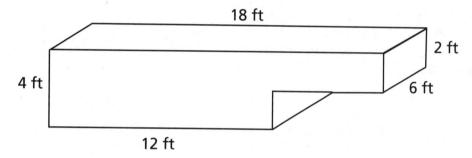

18 ft

2 ft

4 ft

6 ft

12 ft

Show your work.

Answer _____ cubic feet

Solve the problems.

1 Regan wants to convert 2 kilograms to grams. By which number does she need to multiply 2 kilograms?

    A   0.001

    B   0.1

    C   100

    D   1,000

2 Mrs. Davis had 6 bowls of flour for a group project. The line plot shows what fraction of a cup of flour was left in each bowl after the project.

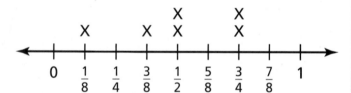

What is the total amount of flour left in the bowls after the project?

    A   4 cups

    B   3 cups

    C $\frac{1}{2}$ cup

    D $\frac{13}{28}$ cup

3 The solid figure below is made up of two rectangular prisms.

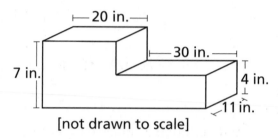

[not drawn to scale]

What is the total volume of the solid figure?

    A   5,170 cubic inches

    B   2,970 cubic inches

    C   2,860 cubic inches

    D   1,980 cubic inches

4 Kyle has an aquarium in the shape of a rectangular prism. The aquarium is 24 inches long and 10 inches wide. The volume of the aquarium is 2,880 cubic inches. How tall is the aquarium?

_____ inches

5 Which measurement is equivalent to 84 inches? Circle the letter for all that apply.

    A   8 feet

    B   1 yard, 2 feet, 24 inches

    C   7 feet

    D $2\frac{1}{3}$ yards

    E   4 feet, 40 inches

6 Bill and Harry are practicing for a track meet. Last week, Bill ran 900 meters on each of 3 days. Harry ran 1.2 kilometers on each of 2 days.

Part A

Which boy ran farther last week and by how much?

Show your work.

_____

Part B

Between last week and this week, Bill wants to run a total of 6 kilometers. How far does Bill need to run this week?

Show your work.

Answer _____ kilometers

7 The figure below is a rectangular prism.

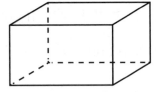

Explain how you can use the area of the base to find the volume of a rectangular prism.

_____

_____

_____

_____

Performance Task

Answer the questions and show all your work on separate paper.

Jack wants to make a terrarium for the science fair. The first steps of the instructions are shown below.

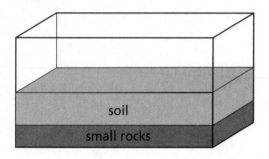

HOW TO MAKE A TERRARIUM

Step 1: Fill the bottom of the tank with a 2-inch layer of small rocks.

Step 2: Add a layer of soil. There should be 5 inches from the top of the soil to the top of the tank.

☑ **CHECKLIST**

Did you . . .

☐ Draw a diagram?

☐ Convert the units?

☐ Use a formula?

Jack already has one cubic foot (1,728 in.^{3}) of soil and $\frac{1}{3}$ cubic foot (576 in.^{3}) of small rocks to use. Now he has to buy a tank. Which of the tanks below can he use without having to buy more rocks and soil?

Tank A: $1\frac{1}{2}$ feet long, 15 inches wide, 15 inches tall

Tank B: 2 feet long, 1 foot wide, 1 foot tall

Tank C: 21 inches long, 18 inches wide, 10 inches tall

Reflect on Mathematical Practices

After you complete the task, choose one of the following questions to answer.

1. **Be Precise** How did you decide which units to use to figure out the amount of rocks and soil needed for each tank?

2. **Model** How does drawing and labeling a diagram help you solve the problem?

Unit 5
Geometry

The question "Where is it?" comes up a lot. You may need to find the subway station at the corner of 23rd Street and Broadway in New York City. A sailor may need to navigate to North 45° West 59° to find another ship off the coast of Canada. In chess, you can move your pawn from c2 to c4 on the chess board. These are all examples of coordinates.

In this unit, you will learn to locate points on a coordinate plane and use what you know about coordinates to solve problems. You will also study some two-dimensional figures and sort them into different categories according to their side lengths, angles, and other properties.

✓ Self Check

Before starting this unit, check off the skills you know below. As you complete each lesson, see how many more you can check off!

I can:	Before this unit	After this unit
graph points in the first quadrant of the coordinate plane	☐	☐
find the distance between two points on the coordinate plane	☐	☐
graph real-world situations on the coordinate plane and interpret the meaning of the graph	☐	☐
classify two-dimensional figures based on their properties, for example: a square is also a rhombus or rectangle, but not all rhombuses and rectangles are squares	☐	☐

What is the coordinate plane?

The **coordinate plane** is a two-dimensional space formed by two perpendicular number lines called axes. Pairs of numbers such as the relationship between the number of days a book is overdue and the amount owed for the library fine.

In the past, you used a number line to represent different numbers. A coordinate plane is made up of two perpendicular number lines that are used to represent pairs of numbers.

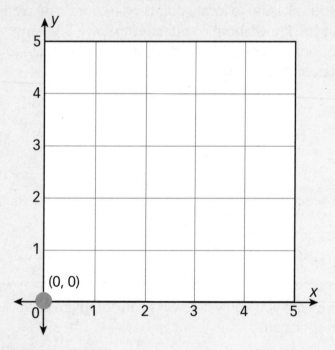

🔍 **Think** How do we distinguish between the two lines?

Look at the horizontal number line in the coordinate plane above. Notice that it is labeled *x*. This line is the **x-axis**. If there is more than one axis, use the term **axes**.

The vertical number line in the coordinate plane is labeled *y*. This line is the **y-axis**.

In this coordinate plane, the axes meet at 0. Notice that the vertical grid lines are labeled with whole numbers on the *x*-axis, and the horizontal grid lines are labeled with the same whole numbers on the *y*-axis.

> **Circle the label on the x-axis, then trace the x-axis with your finger. Do the same with the y-axis.**

🔍 **Think** What does it mean when the axes intersect?

Look at the coordinate plane. Notice the 0 labeled at the point where the *x*-axis and *y*-axis cross.

The point where the axes meet is the **origin**. Write "origin" next to this point. The origin on the coordinate plane is the starting point for the whole numbers on the two axes.

The origin is a point named with two numbers, 0 and 0, which you label (0, 0). This **ordered pair** represents the location where the lines meet. It also tells how far the point is from the origin in both directions.

> *The axes meet at point (0, 0). I wonder if the other numbers on the axes are used to name other points where lines meet.*

This table summarizes some of the new terms you should know to help you understand the coordinate plane.

Term	Definition
coordinate plane	a two-dimensional space formed by two perpendicular number lines called axes
x-axis	the horizontal number line
y-axis	the vertical number line
origin	the point (0, 0) where the *x*-axis and *y*-axis intersect
ordered pair	a pair of numbers, or coordinates (*x*, *y*), describing the location of a point on the coordinate plane
x-coordinate	distance from the origin along the *x*-axis
y-coordinate	distance from the origin along the *y*-axis

✏️ **Reflect**

1 What other words sound like "origin"? What do these words mean?

_____

_____

_____

Explore It

A coordinate plane is used to represent ordered pairs of numbers with points. The origin is point (0, 0).

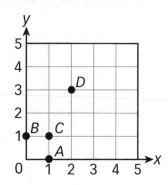

2 The first number in an ordered pair is the x-coordinate. Starting at the y-axis, point D is how many units from the origin? _____ Write this as the first number in the ordered pair.

Ordered Pair for point D
$(x, y) \longrightarrow$ (_____ , _____)

3 The second number in an ordered pair is the y-coordinate. Starting at the x-axis, point D is how many units from the origin? _____ Write this as the second number in the ordered pair.

4 Locate point A. Starting at the y-axis, point A is how many units from the origin?

_____ unit(s)

Starting at the x-axis, point A is how many units from the origin? _____ unit(s)

The ordered pair for point A is (_____ , _____).

5 Locate point B. Identify the ordered pair for point B. (_____ , _____)

6 Identify the ordered pair for point C. (_____ , _____)

7 How did you determine the coordinates for the ordered pairs? _____

_____

_____

Talk About It

Solve the problems below as a group.

Use the coordinate plane from the previous page. Now you will describe the points as movements from the origin.

8 Place your finger on the origin. Move right and up to point *D*. Use words to describe how far to the right and up point *D* is from (0, 0). _____

_____

How is the location of point *D* related to the ordered pair (2, 3)? _____

_____

9 Start at (0, 0). Move to point *A*. How is your move related to the ordered pair (1, 0)?

_____

_____

10 How do you move from the origin to the ordered pair (0, 1)? Move right _____ units and move _____   _____ unit.

What point did you end on? _____

11 The ordered pair (1, 1) means to move right _____ unit(s) and up _____ unit(s). What letter represents this point on the coordinate plane? _____

12 Find the ordered pair (3, 2) on the coordinate plane. Label this point "*E*".

Try It Another Way

Work with your group to show ordered pairs on the coordinate plane.

13 Complete the table to show the ordered pairs.

Point	A	B	C	D	E	F
x	1					4
y	0					0

14 Find and label point *F* on the coordinate plane to represent the ordered pair shown in the table.

Connect It

Talk through these problems as a class. Then write your answers below.

15 Show: Look at the table below. Mark and label points *M* and *N* on the coordinate plane. Then write ordered pairs for the points and describe how to move from (0, 0) to get to each point.

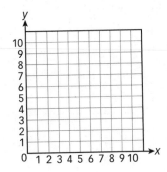

Point	x	y
M	1	4
N	5	2

_____

_____

16 Analyze: Irvin identified the ordered pair for point *J* on the coordinate plane as (4, 3). Explain what is wrong with Irvin's ordered pair.

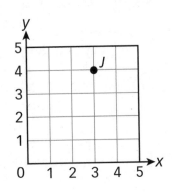

_____

_____

_____

17 Create: Choose 3 points and draw a triangle on the coordinate plane. Label the points with letters.

Below, write the letters and ordered pairs you used to draw your triangle.

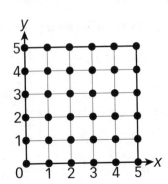

_____

_____

_____

🔍 Put It Together

18 Use what you have learned to complete this task.

A Use the coordinate plane below to complete the *x-y* table.

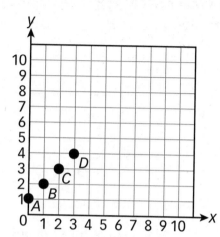

Point	x	y
A		
B		
C		
D		

B Identify a pattern you see represented by the points in the table and a pattern you see represented by the points on the coordinate plane.

_____

_____

_____

_____

C Name and plot 3 other points that follow this pattern.

_____

Lesson 29   Part 1: Introduction 👥

Graph Points in the Coordinate Plane

In Lesson 28, you learned about the coordinate plane. Now you will use and graph points to solve problems. Take a look at this problem.

The coordinate plane shows the layout of booths at a county fair. There is a booth at each point where the grid lines intersect. Some of the booths are labeled. Meg is at the ring toss booth, and she wants to go to the face-painting booth. Describe two different paths she can take.

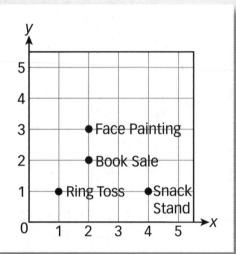

🔍 Explore It

Use the math you already know to solve the problem.

▪ What ordered pair represents the ring toss booth? _____

▪ What ordered pair represents the face-painting booth? _____

▪ Describe one way to move from the ring toss booth to the face-painting booth by first moving to the right. _____

▪ Now describe a different path to get from the ring toss booth to the face-painting booth. _____

🔍 Find Out More

On the previous page, you used the grid to help describe a path. You can also use the ordered pairs to help describe the movement from one point to another on a grid.

Meg moved 1 unit right. This is a move along the *x*-axis. You can look at the change in the *x*-coordinates to describe this move,

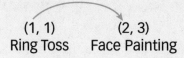

(1, 1)   (2, 3)
Ring Toss   Face Painting

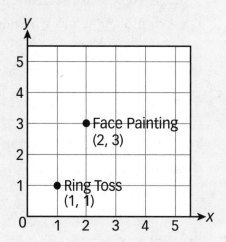

Subtract 2 − 1 to find the change in the *x*-coordinate. This is 1 unit. Since 2 is to the right of 1 on the *x*-axis, the move is 1 unit to the right.

Meg also moved 2 units up. This is a move along the *y*-axis. You can look at the change in the *y*-coordinates to describe this move.

(1, 1)   (2, 3)
Ring Toss   Face Painting

Subtract 3 − 1 to find the change in the *y*-coordinate. This is 2 units. Since 3 is up from 1 on the *x*-axis, the move is 2 units up.

✎ Reflect

1   Pick two other points on the grid on the previous page. Use the coordinates to describe a path from one point to the other.

_____

_____

_____

_____

_____

Read the problem below. Then explore different ways to represent and use relationships between quantities in problems.

Gabe has $8. He goes to an arcade where each game costs $1. On a coordinate plane, represent the relationship between how many games Gabe plays and how much money he has left. How many games can Gabe play if he wants to leave the arcade with $2?

Model It

You can use equations to represent the relationship.

Gabe starts with $8. He spends $1 on each game.

$8 − ($1 × number of games) = money remaining

$8 − ($1 × 1) = $7 remaining

$8 − ($1 × 2) = $6 remaining

$8 − ($1 × 3) = $5 remaining

$8 − ($1 × 4) = $4 remaining

$8 − ($1 × 5) = $3 remaining

$8 − ($1 × 6) = $2 remaining

Model It

You can use a table to model the relationship.

The table shows how much money Gabe has left after he plays different numbers of games.

Number of Games Played	0	1	2	3	4	5	6
Amount of Money Left, $	8	7	6	5	4	3	2

 **Connect It**

Now you will solve the problem from the previous page by representing the relationship between the quantities on a coordinate plane.

2 What quantity in the problem stays the same? _____

What two quantities change? _____

3 What quantity is represented on the *x*-axis? _____

What quantity is represented on the *y*-axis? _____

4 How much money does Gabe have after he plays 0 games? Complete the ordered pair:

    (0 games, $_____)

Plot the point on the coordinate plane.

5 Complete the ordered pairs below:

(1 game, $_____), (2 games, $_____)
(3 games, $_____), (4 games, $_____)
(5 games, $_____), (6 games, $_____)

Plot each ordered pair on the coordinate plane.

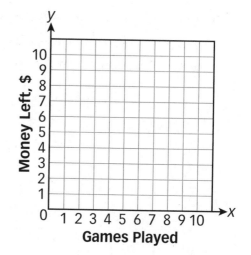

6 What is the meaning of (6, 2)? _____

_____

7 How can you use a graph to represent relationships between two sets of numbers?

_____

✎ **Try It**

Use what you just learned about representing problems on the coordinate plane to solve this problem. Show your work on a separate sheet of paper.

8 Gabe decided to play a game that costs $2 for each round at the arcade. What ordered pairs represent the amount left after playing each game? Use an "X" to mark each point on the coordinate plane above. What is different about this set of points and the solution?

_____

_____

Read the problem below. Then explore different ways of using a graph on the coordinate plane to solve a problem.

Mrs. Sautter writes the following ordered pairs on the board: *M*(2, 1), *A*(2, 5), *T*(5, 5), and *H*(5, 1). The point represented by each ordered pair is a vertex of the rectangle *MATH*. What is the perimeter of the rectangle *MATH*?

Picture It

You can picture the rectangle on a coordinate plane.

Plot the points for the vertices of the rectangle. Connect the points to draw the sides of the rectangle. Then shade the rectangle.

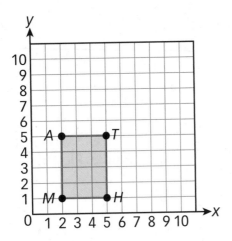

To find the perimeter, count the number of units on each side to find the side lengths. Then add the side lengths: 4 + 3 + 4 + 3 = 14; the perimeter is 14 units.

Model It

You can find the perimeter of any rectangle with a formula.

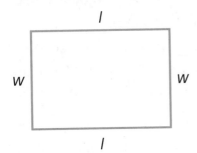

$P = 2l + 2w$ or $P = 2 \times (l + w)$

Connect It

Now you will solve the problem from the previous page using your understanding of distance between two points on a number line.

9 What are the coordinate pairs for points *A* and *T*? _____

Which are different, the *x*-coordinates or *y*-coordinates? _____

Write an expression to show the distance between the two different coordinates. _____

What is the length of $\overline{AT}$? _____ units

10 Consider how you found the length of $\overline{AT}$ above.

What is the length of $\overline{MA}$? _____ units

Explain how you found this length. _____

_____

11 What is the perimeter of the rectangle? _____ units

Explain how you found the perimeter. _____

_____

12 How can you find the vertical distance between two points?

_____

13 How can you find the horizontal distance between two points?

_____

Try It

Use what you just learned about finding the distance between two points to solve these problems. Show your work on another sheet of paper.

14 What is the distance between the *y*-coordinates of (3, 8) and (3, 4)? _____

15 What is the distance between the *x*-coordinates of (4, 2) and (4, 5)? _____

Study the solution below. Then solve problems 16–18.

The labels on the axes tell me what the numbers mean.

Pair/Share

Explain how to use the graph to find how many chores Jaina must complete to earn $4.

Student Model

The graph shows how Jaina's parents determine her weekly allowance. What is the meaning of (3, 5)?

Look at how you can use the graph to solve this problem.

The *x*-axis is labeled "Chores Completed." The *x*-coordinate in (3, 5) is 3. The *y*-axis is labeled "Weekly Allowance." The *y*-coordinate in (3, 5) is 5.

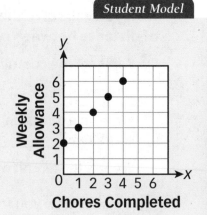

Solution: ___If Jaina completes 3 chores, she will earn $5.___

Do parallel lines ever intersect?

16 Plot the points (4, 4), (8, 4), (3, 1), and (7, 1) on the coordinate plane. Use the points to draw two parallel, horizontal segments. Label the endpoints of one segment *A* and *B*. Label the endpoints of the other segment *C* and *D*. What is the distance between each pair of points?

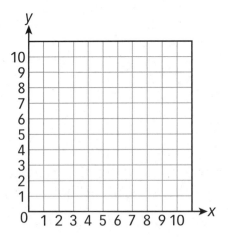

Pair/Share

What shape could have the 4 points as vertices? Draw the shape on the coordinate plane.

Solution: _____

_____

17 What is the area of rectangle *EFGH* shown on the coordinate plane?

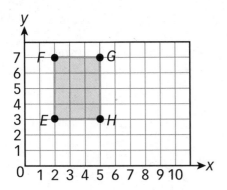

Show your work.

 The formula for the area of a rectangle is A = l × w.

Solution: _____

Pair/Share

Suppose the x-coordinates for points G and H each increase by 1. What kind of shape would this be? What is the area?

18 Mr. Palmer uses a coordinate plane to design his bulletin board.

He moves Rules 2 units right and 3 units down. What ordered pair represents the new location of the rules? Circle the letter of the correct answer.

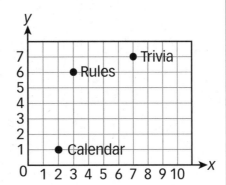

A (5, 3)

B (1, 9)

C (1, 3)

D (5, 9)

Maya chose **C** as the correct answer. How did she get that answer?

_____

_____

_____

What is the ordered pair for the starting point? For the ending point?

Pair/Share

Does Maya's answer make sense?

Solve the problems.

1 Look at triangle *ABC*.

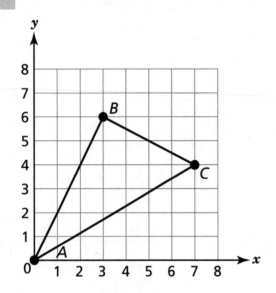

What are the coordinates of *A*, *B*, and *C*?

A   *A*(1, 1), *B*(6, 3), *C*(4, 7)

B   *A*(1, 1), *B*(3, 6), *C*(7, 4)

C   *A*(0, 0), *B*(6, 3), *C*(4, 7)

D   *A*(0, 0), *B*(3, 6), *C*(7, 4)

2 The coordinate plane below shows rhombus *RHOM* with lines of symmetry.

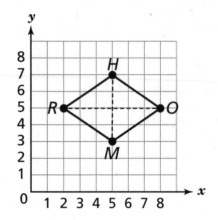

What is the length of $\overline{RO}$?

_____ units

3 Plot the following three points on the coordinate plane.

(2, 5)   (7, 3)   (4, 0)

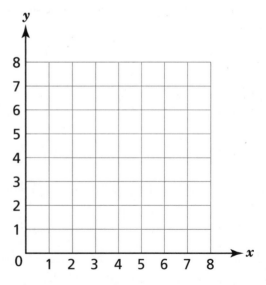

4   The coordinate plane shows how much water is in a bathtub after the faucet is turned on.

How many minutes must the faucet be turned on for the bathtub to hold 8 gallons of water?

A   16 minutes

B   8 minutes

C   4 minutes

D   2 minutes

FILLING BATHTUB

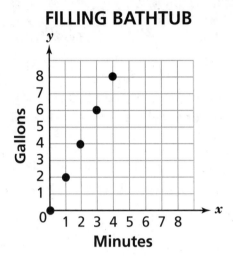

5

Part A

The area of rectangle *RSTU* is 20 square units. Draw rectangle *RSTU* with a vertex at the origin on the coordinate plane below.

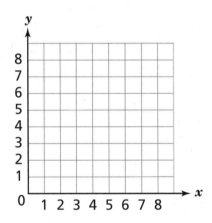

Part B

Write the ordered pairs of *R, S, T,* and *U.* _____

Part C

How do you know the area of rectangle *RSTU* is 20 square units?

_____

_____

 **Self Check**   *Go back and see what you can check off on the Self Check on page 251.*

Lesson 30 Part 1: Introduction 👥
Classify Two-Dimensional Figures

In this lesson, you will classify polygons by their properties such as sides and angles. Take a look at this problem.

Arrange the polygons below so that a polygon can also be called by the name of the polygon before it. Order them from left to right.

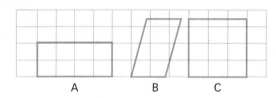

A   B   C

🔍 Explore It

Use the math you already know to solve the problem.

▪ What are the properties of polygon A? _____

_____

Circle all the names that polygon A can be called.

    quadrilateral   parallelogram   rectangle   square

▪ What are the properties of polygon B? _____

Circle all the names that polygon B can be called.

    quadrilateral   parallelogram   rectangle   square

▪ What are the properties of polygon C? _____

_____

Circle all the names that polygon C can be called.

    quadrilateral   parallelogram   rectangle   square

▪ Write the most specific name for each polygon shown above.

    A: _____   B: _____   C: _____

▪ How can you order the polygons so that each can also be called by the name of the ones before it? _____

🔍 Find Out More

When you order categories of shapes by their properties, you put them in a **hierarchy**. A hierarchy starts with the most general group. Then it shows how more specific groups are related.

A Venn diagram can show categories and subcategories. This Venn diagram shows that parallelograms have all the properties that quadrilaterals have and some new ones. Rectangles have all the properties that parallelograms have and some new ones. Squares have all the properties that rectangles have and some new ones.

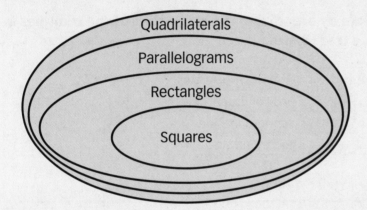

A flow chart also can show the hierarchy of the categories and subcategories of shapes. The most general category is at the left, while the most specific is at the right. This flow chart shows the three quadrilaterals from the most general to the most specific.

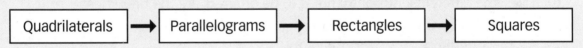

✏️ Reflect

1 How are the flow chart and the Venn diagram alike? How are they different?

_____

_____

_____

_____

Read the problem below. Then explore different ways to understand ordering shapes in a hierarchy.

Order the following triangles from the most general to the most specific: scalene triangle, isosceles triangle, and equilateral triangle. Use a tree diagram to order them.

 **Model It**

You can understand the problem by organizing the properties of the triangles in a table before ordering them in a tree diagram.

Triangle	Side Properties
Isosceles	2 or 3 congruent sides
Scalene	no congruent sides
Equilateral	3 congruent sides

Model It

You can represent the problem by starting a tree diagram of the triangles.

A tree diagram can show the hierarchy of the categories and subcategories of shapes. The most general category, triangles, is the top box of the tree. The subcategories of triangles, the different kinds of triangles to be ordered, are the branches.

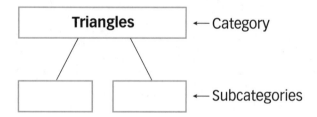

Connect It

Now you will solve the problem from the previous page using the tree diagram and the shared properties of the triangles from the table.

2 Why is "Triangles" in the top row of the tree diagram? _____

_____

3 Write "Scalene" and "Isosceles" in the second row of the tree diagram.

Why can their categories NOT overlap?

_____

_____

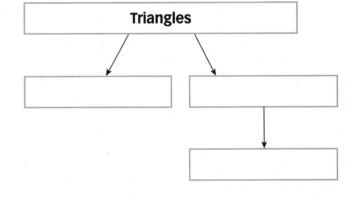

4 Write "Equilateral" beneath "Isosceles."

Why can all equilateral triangles be classified as isosceles?

_____

5 How can you use a tree diagram to order shapes? _____

_____

Try It

Use what you learned about ordering shapes in a hierarchy to solve this problem.

6 Complete the Venn diagram below to show the hierarchy of isosceles, scalene, and equilateral triangles.

Triangles

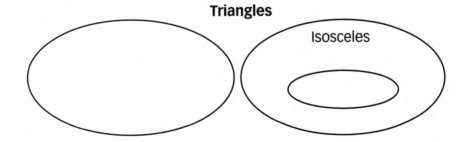

Study the model below. Then solve problems 7–9.

Categories that can never overlap, like hexagons and quadrilaterals, are shown as separate circles.

Create a Venn diagram to show the hierarchy of quadrilaterals, polygons, trapezoids, and hexagons.

Look at how you could show your work using a Venn diagram.

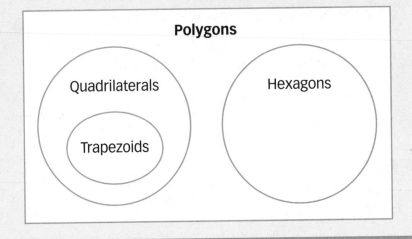

Polygons

Quadrilaterals

Hexagons

Trapezoids

Pair/Share

Recreate the hierarchy with a tree diagram.

Which type of triangle is the most specific?

7 Look at the tree diagram below. Write a statement about the relationship between acute triangles and equilateral triangles.

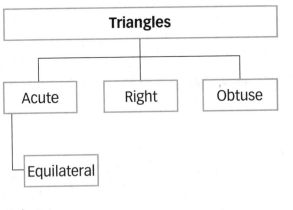

Triangles

Acute

Right

Obtuse

Equilateral

Solution: _____

_____

Pair/Share

Write a statement about the relationship between acute triangles and obtuse triangles.

8 Create a Venn diagram to show the ranking of the polygons described in the chart.

Shape	Description
Trapezoid	quadrilateral with at least 1 pair of parallel sides
Isosceles trapezoid	trapezoid with at least 2 congruent sides
Parallelogram	quadrilateral with 2 pairs of parallel sides

"At least 2" means 2 or more.

🗨**Pair/Share**

Draw one example of a polygon in each separate category of your Venn diagram.

9 Look at the flow chart below.

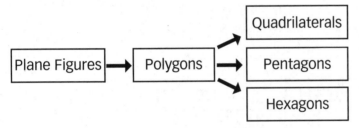

Which statement is true? Circle the letter of the correct answer.

A A plane figure will always be a polygon.

B All polygons are plane figures.

C A polygon is always a quadrilateral, a pentagon, or a hexagon.

D A hexagon is not a plane figure.

Brad chose **C** as the correct answer. How did he get that answer?

_____

_____

_____

The flow chart is like a tree diagram. But the arrows show that the ranking moves from left to right instead of top to bottom.

🗨**Pair/Share**

Does Brad's answer make sense?

Solve the problems.

1 Look at the shape below.

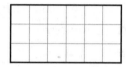

Which is a correct classification for this shape from LEAST specific to MOST specific?

A polygon, quadrilateral, rectangle

B quadrilateral, parallelogram, square

C polygon, quadrilateral, rhombus

D quadrilateral, rectangle, square

2 Classify the triangles as scalene, isosceles, or obtuse. Draw the triangles in the correct box of the table. If a triangle fits more than one classification, draw it in all the boxes that apply. If none of these classifications apply, leave it outside the boxes.

SCALENE	ISOSCELES	OBTUSE

3   The word "isosceles" can be used to describe any polygon with at least 2 congruent sides.

Look at the following flow chart.

Part A

Draw an example of an isosceles trapezoid.

Part B

Explain how isosceles trapezoids relate to parallelograms.

_____

_____

_____

Part C

Can you use the term isosceles to describe a rectangle? Explain your reasoning.

_____

_____

✓ **Self Check**   *Go back and see what you can check off on the Self Check on page 251.*

Lesson 31   Part 1: Introduction 👥
Understand Properties of Two-Dimensional Figures

CCSS
5.G.B.3

> **How do we group polygons into categories?**

Polygons are grouped into categories by their **attributes**, such as the number of sides or angles, the side lengths, and the angle measures. All polygons in the same category share certain attributes. Some attributes of polygons are described in the table below.

Polygon Attribute	Description	Example
Scalene	No congruent sides	
Isosceles	At least 2 congruent sides	
Equilateral	All congruent sides	
Regular	All congruent sides	
Irregular	At least 1 side and 1 interior angle are not congruent to the others	
Right	At least 1 pair of perpendicular sides	
Parallel sides	At least 1 pair of opposite sides, if extended forever, will never intersect	

🔍 **Think**   Can a polygon be categorized in more than 1 way?

Think about how a quadrilateral is defined. It is a polygon with 4 sides. So any shape with 4 straight sides can be called both a polygon and a quadrilateral. If the quadrilateral has two pairs of parallel sides, then it can also be called a parallelogram.

Every parallelogram is a quadrilateral because every parallelogram has 4 sides. But not all quadrilaterals are parallelograms because not all quadrilaterals have two pairs of parallel sides.

> **Shade a polygon above that can be named both a quadrilateral and parallelogram.**

Part 1: Introduction

🔍 **Think** How can we show the relationships among polygons with a diagram?

A Venn diagram is a useful tool for organizing categories of polygons that share characteristics.

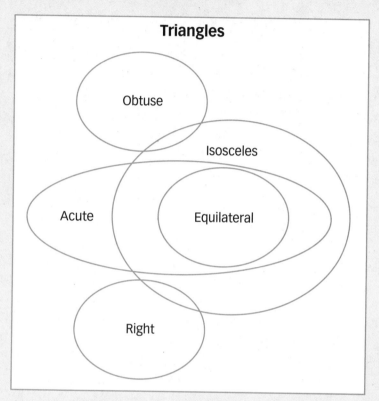

The Venn diagram shows me that right triangles never overlap with equilateral triangles.

Notice that Right partly overlaps Isosceles. A right triangle can share all the properties of an isosceles triangle. Also notice that Right does not overlap Obtuse. A right triangle will never share all the properties of an obtuse triangle.

The category for equilateral triangles is nested completely inside the category for isosceles triangles to show that it shares all of the same properties and is a subcategory of isosceles triangles.

✏️ **Reflect**

1 What do you learn from the diagram showing that the space for obtuse triangles partly overlaps the space for isosceles triangles?

_____

_____

_____

Explore It

A Venn diagram can help you understand what properties are shared by categories of polygons.

2 The Venn diagram shows categories of quadrilaterals with different properties. Write the name of each category that fits the description.

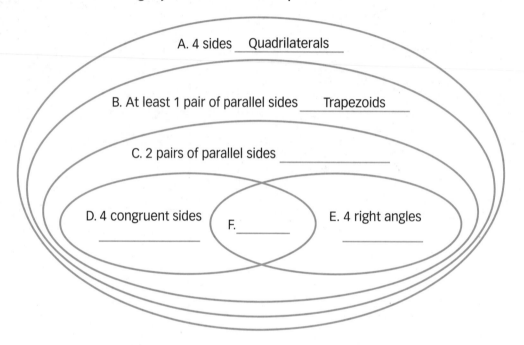

A. 4 sides ___Quadrilaterals___

B. At least 1 pair of parallel sides ___Trapezoids___

C. 2 pairs of parallel sides _____

D. 4 congruent sides _____   F. _____   E. 4 right angles _____

3 Use the Venn diagram to fill in the table below.

Category	Properties	Name
A	4 sides	quadrilateral
B	4 sides, at least 1 pair of parallel sides	trapezoid
C	4 sides, 2 pairs of parallel sides	
D	4 sides, 2 pairs of parallel sides, 4 congruent sides	
E		
F		

🗨 Talk About It

Use the Venn diagram to help you understand how properties are shared by categories of quadrilaterals.

4 Is every property of parallelograms also a property of all rectangles? _____

Is every property of rectangles also a property of all parallelograms? _____

Explain what the Venn diagram shows about the relationship between rectangles and parallelograms. _____

_____

Classify each inference statement as true or false. If false, explain.

5 The opposite angles of any parallelogram are congruent. Therefore, the opposite angles of any rhombus are congruent. _____

_____

6 The diagonals of any square are congruent. Therefore, the diagonals of any rhombus are congruent. _____

_____

✎ Try It Another Way

The flow chart below shows another way to think about how quadrilaterals are categorized and ranked.

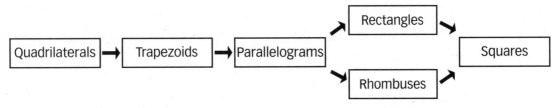

Use the flow chart to describe the statements as true or false:

7 The diagonals of a rectangle are congruent. Therefore, the diagonals of any parallelogram must be congruent. _____

8 A rhombus has 2 lines of symmetry. Therefore, a square has 2 lines of symmetry.

_____

Connect It

Talk through these problems as a class. Then write your answers below.

9 **Categorize:** Polygons are either **convex** or **concave**. A convex polygon has all interior angles less than 180°. A triangle is an example. A concave polygon has at least 1 interior angle greater than 180°. The quadrilateral below is an example.

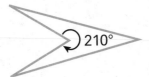
210°

Categorize concave polygons, convex polygons, triangles, quadrilaterals, and rectangles in a Venn diagram. Draw an example of each polygon in the diagram.

10 **Explain:** Nadriette said that a rectangle can never be called a trapezoid. Explain what is incorrect with Nadriette's statement. _____

_____

11 **Create:** Describe the properties of a shape that is both a rectangle and a rhombus. Draw an example.

_____

🔍 **Put It Together**

12 Use what you just learned about classifying polygons to complete this task.

A Create a tree diagram to show the following types of triangles: acute, obtuse, right, isosceles, and equilateral. Use information in the table to help you.

Triangle	Angle Properties
Acute	all acute angles
Right	2 acute angles and 1 angle exactly 90°
Obtuse	2 acute angles and 1 obtuse angle
Scalene	acute, right, or obtuse
Isosceles	acute, right, or obtuse
Equilateral	all acute angles

B Write a statement that is always true about the relationship between obtuse triangles and equilateral triangles.

_____

_____

C Write a statement that is sometimes true about the relationship between acute triangles and isosceles triangles.

_____

_____

Solve the problems.

1 Jack, Chris, Ryan, Peter, and Sam all attend Laurelleaf Elementary School. The map shows where their houses are in relation to the school.

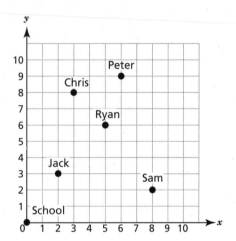

What *x*-coordinate helps describe the location of Ryan's house?

A	2	**C**	5
B	3	**D**	6

2 Which figure is a rectangle?

A

B

C

D

3 Look at rectangle *ABCD* on the coordinate plane.

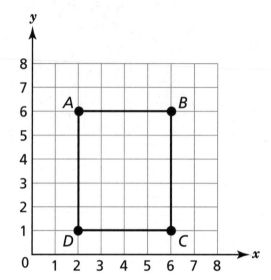

Choose *True* or *False* for each statement.

A The coordinates of point *A* are (6, 2).

☐ True   ☐ False

B The coordinates of point *D* are (2, 1).

☐ True   ☐ False

C The area of rectangle *ABCD* is 36 square units.

☐ True   ☐ False

D The perimeter of rectangle *ABCD* is 18 units.

☐ True   ☐ False

4 Which statement is true based on the diagram? Circle the letter for all that apply.

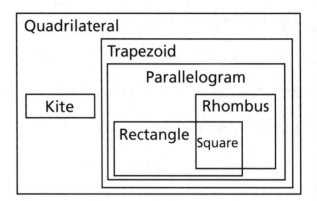

   A   All parallelograms are trapezoids.

   B   All rectangles are squares.

   C   All quadrilaterals are parallelograms.

   D   All squares are parallelograms.

   E   All polygons are quadrilaterals.

5

Part A

Circle the quadrilaterals below that are rectangles.

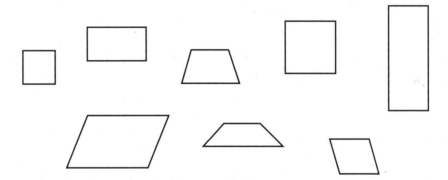

Part B

The table shows the attributes of parallelograms and rhombuses.

All parallelograms have:	All rhombuses have:
4 sides	4 congruent sides
4 vertices	4 vertices
2 pairs of parallel sides	2 pairs of parallel sides

Using the information in the table, complete the sentence below.

All _____ are _____ , but not all _____ are _____ .

Performance Task

Answer the questions and show all your work on separate paper.

Ben and Cari are trying to solve the puzzle below.

Name That Shape

1. The figure is a quadrilateral.

2. The figure has a pair of parallel sides.

3. Three of the vertices are located at (1, 2), (3, 5), and (7, 5) on a coordinate plane.

What type of figure is it? Where is the last vertex?

Ben thinks there's just one solution to the puzzle. Cari says there's more than one possible answer. Who do you think is right? Explain your reasoning. Then solve the puzzle. If you agree with Cari, find at least two possibilities for the fourth vertex.

Create your own geometry puzzle with 3 clues. Make sure your puzzle has only one answer and that it cannot be answered with only the first 2 clues.

Reflect on Mathematical Practices

After you complete the task, choose one of the following questions to answer.

1. **Use Structure** How did you use the clues to solve the puzzle?

2. **Be Precise** What did you think about when writing your own puzzle?

Common Core State Standards for Mathematics, Grade 5

The chart below correlates each Common Core State Standard to the *Ready® Common Core Instruction* lesson(s) that offer(s) comprehensive instruction on that standard. Use this chart to determine which lessons your students should complete based on their mastery of each standard.

Common Core State Standards for Grade 5 Mathematics — Standards for Mathematical Content	Content Emphasis	Ready® Common Core Instruction Lesson(s)
Operations and Algebraic Thinking		
Write and interpret numerical expressions.		
5.OA.A.1 Use parentheses, brackets, or braces in numerical expressions, and evaluate expressions with these symbols.	Supporting/ Additional	19
5.OA.A.2 Write simple expressions that record calculations with numbers, and interpret numerical expressions without evaluating them. *For example, express the calculation "add 8 and 7, then multiply by 2" as $2 \times (8 + 7)$. Recognize that $3 \times (18932 + 921)$ is three times as large as $18932 + 921$, without having to calculate the indicated sum or product.*	Supporting/ Additional	19
Analyze patterns and relationships.		
5.OA.B.3 Generate two numerical patterns using two given rules. Identify apparent relationships between corresponding terms. Form ordered pairs consisting of corresponding terms from the two patterns, and graph the ordered pairs on a coordinate plane. *For example, given the rule "Add 3" and the starting number 0, and given the rule "Add 6" and the starting number 0, generate terms in the resulting sequences, and observe that the terms in one sequence are twice the corresponding terms in the other sequence. Explain informally why this is so.*	Supporting/ Additional	20
Number and Operations in Base Ten		
Understand the place value system.		
5.NBT.A.1 Recognize that in a multi-digit number, a digit in one place represents 10 times as much as it represents in the place to its right and $\frac{1}{10}$ of what it represents in the place to its left.	Major	1
5.NBT.A.2 Explain patterns in the number of zeros of the product when multiplying a number by powers of 10, and explain patterns in the placement of the decimal point when a decimal is multiplied or divided by a power of 10. Use whole-number exponents to denote powers of 10.	Major	2
5.NBT.A.3 Read, write, and compare decimals to thousandths.	Major	3, 4
5.NBT.A.3a Read and write decimals to thousandths using base-ten numerals, number names, and expanded form, e.g., $347.392 = 3 \times 100 + 4 \times 10 + 7 \times 1 + 3 \times \left(\frac{1}{10}\right) + 9 \times \left(\frac{1}{100}\right) + 2 \times \left(\frac{1}{1000}\right)$.	Major	3
5.NBT.A.3b Compare two decimals to thousandths based on meanings of the digits in each place, using $>$, $=$, and $<$ symbols to record the results of comparisons.	Major	4
5.NBT.A.4 Use place value understanding to round decimals to any place.	Major	4
Perform operations with multi-digit whole numbers and with decimals to hundredths.		
5.NBT.B.5 Fluently multiply multi-digit whole numbers using the standard algorithm.	Major	5
5.NBT.B.6 Find whole-number quotients of whole numbers with up to four-digit dividends and two-digit divisors, using strategies based on place value, the properties of operations, and/or the relationship between multiplication and division. Illustrate and explain the calculation by using equations, rectangular arrays, and/or area models.	Major	6
5.NBT.B.7 Add, subtract, multiply, and divide decimals to hundredths, using concrete models or drawings and strategies based on place value, properties of operations, and/or the relationship between addition and subtraction; relate the strategy to a written method and explain the reasoning used.	Major	7, 8, 9

The Standards for Mathematical Practice are integrated throughout the instructional lessons.

©2010. National Governors Association Center for Best Practices and Council of Chief State School Officers. All rights reserved.

Common Core State Standards for Grade 5 Mathematics — Standards for Mathematical Content	Content Emphasis	*Ready®* Common Core Instruction Lesson(s)

Number and Operations—Fractions

Use equivalent fractions as a strategy to add and subtract fractions.

5.NF.A.1 Add and subtract fractions with unlike denominators (including mixed numbers) by replacing given fractions with equivalent fractions in such a way as to produce an equivalent sum or difference of fractions with like denominators. *For example,* $\frac{2}{3} + \frac{5}{4} = \frac{8}{12} + \frac{15}{12} = \frac{23}{12}$. (*In general,* $\frac{a}{b} + \frac{c}{d} = \frac{(ad + bc)}{bd}$.)	Major	10
5.NF.A.2 Solve word problems involving addition and subtraction of fractions referring to the same whole, including cases of unlike denominators, e.g., by using visual fraction models or equations to represent the problem. Use benchmark fractions and number sense of fractions to estimate mentally and assess the reasonableness of answers. *For example, recognize an incorrect result* $\frac{2}{5} + \frac{1}{2} = \frac{3}{7}$, *by observing that* $\frac{3}{7} < \frac{1}{2}$.	Major	11

Apply and extend previous understandings of multiplication and division.

5.NF.B.3 Interpret a fraction as division of the numerator by the denominator $\left(\frac{a}{b} = a \div b\right)$. Solve word problems involving division of whole numbers leading to answers in the form of fractions or mixed numbers, e.g., by using visual fraction models or equations to represent the problem. *For example, interpret* $\frac{3}{4}$ *as the result of dividing 3 by 4, noting that* $\frac{3}{4}$ *multiplied by 4 equals 3, and that when 3 wholes are shared equally among 4 people each person has a share of size* $\frac{3}{4}$. *If 9 people want to share a 50-pound sack of rice equally by weight, how many pounds of rice should each person get? Between what two whole numbers does your answer lie?*	Major	12
5.NF.B.4 Apply and extend previous understandings of multiplication to multiply a fraction or whole number by a fraction.	Major	13, 14
5.NF.B.4a Interpret the product $\left(\frac{a}{b}\right) \times q$ as a parts of a partition of q into b equal parts; equivalently, as the result of a sequence of operations $a \times q \div b$. *For example, use a visual fraction model to show* $\left(\frac{2}{3}\right) \times 4 = \frac{8}{3}$, *and create a story context for this equation. Do the same with* $\left(\frac{2}{3}\right) \times \left(\frac{4}{5}\right) = \frac{8}{15}$. (*In general,* $\left(\frac{a}{b}\right) \times \left(\frac{c}{d}\right) = \frac{ac}{bd}$.)	Major	13
5.NF.B.4b Find the area of a rectangle with fractional side lengths by tiling it with unit squares of the appropriate unit fraction side lengths, and show that the area is the same as would be found by multiplying the side lengths. Multiply fractional side lengths to find areas of rectangles, and represent fraction products as rectangular areas.	Major	14
5.NF.B.5 Interpret multiplication as scaling (resizing), by:	Major	15
5.NF.B.5a Comparing the size of a product to the size of one factor on the basis of the size of the other factor, without performing the indicated multiplication.	Major	15
5.NF.B.5b Explaining why multiplying a given number by a fraction greater than 1 results in a product greater than the given number (recognizing multiplication by whole numbers greater than 1 as a familiar case); explaining why multiplying a given number by a fraction less than 1 results in a product smaller than the given number; and relating the principle of fraction equivalence $\frac{a}{b} = \frac{(n \times a)}{(n \times b)}$ to the effect of multiplying $\frac{a}{b}$ by 1.	Major	15
5.NF.B.6 Solve real world problems involving multiplication of fractions and mixed numbers, e.g., by using visual fraction models or equations to represent the problem.	Major	16
5.NF.B.7 Apply and extend previous understandings of division to divide unit fractions by whole numbers and whole numbers by unit fractions.[1]	Major	17, 18

[1] Students able to multiply fractions in general can develop strategies to divide fractions in general, by reasoning about the relationship between multiplication and division. But division of a fraction by a fraction is not a requirement at this grade.

The Standards for Mathematical Practice are integrated throughout the instructional lessons.

Common Core State Standards for Grade 5 Mathematics — Standards for Mathematical Content	Content Emphasis	Ready® Common Core Instruction Lesson(s)

Number and Operations—Fractions (continued)

Apply and extend previous understandings of multiplication and division. (continued)

	Content Emphasis	Lesson(s)
5.NF.B.7a Interpret division of a unit fraction by a non-zero whole number, and compute such quotients. *For example, create a story context for $\left(\frac{1}{3}\right) \div 4$, and use a visual fraction model to show the quotient. Use the relationship between multiplication and division to explain that $\left(\frac{1}{3}\right) \div 4 = \frac{1}{12}$ because $\left(\frac{1}{12}\right) \times 4 = \frac{1}{3}$.*	Major	17
5.NF.B.7b Interpret division of a whole number by a unit fraction, and compute such quotients. *For example, create a story context for $4 \div \left(\frac{1}{5}\right)$, and use a visual fraction model to show the quotient. Use the relationship between multiplication and division to explain that $4 \div \left(\frac{1}{5}\right) = 20$ because $20 \times \left(\frac{1}{5}\right) = 4$.*	Major	17
5.NF.B.7c Solve real world problems involving division of unit fractions by non-zero whole numbers and division of whole numbers by unit fractions, e.g., by using visual fraction models and equations to represent the problem. *For example, how much chocolate will each person get if 3 people share $\frac{1}{2}$ lb of chocolate equally? How many $\frac{1}{3}$-cup servings are in 2 cups of raisins?*	Major	18

Measurement and Data

Convert like measurement units within a given measurement system.

	Content Emphasis	Lesson(s)
5.MD.A.1 Convert among different-sized standard measurement units within a given measurement system (e.g., convert 5 cm to 0.05 m), and use these conversions in solving multi-step, real world problems.	Supporting/ Additional	21, 22

Represent and interpret data.

	Content Emphasis	Lesson(s)
5.MD.B.2 Make a line plot to display a data set of measurements in fractions of a unit $\left(\frac{1}{2}, \frac{1}{4}, \frac{1}{8}\right)$. Use operations on fractions for this grade to solve problems involving information presented in line plots. *For example, given different measurements of liquid in identical beakers, find the amount of liquid each beaker would contain if the total amount in all the beakers were redistributed equally.*	Supporting/ Additional	23

Geometric measurement: understand concepts of volume.

	Content Emphasis	Lesson(s)
5.MD.C.3 Recognize volume as an attribute of solid figures and understand concepts of volume measurement.	Major	24
5.MD.C.3a A cube with side length 1 unit, called a "unit cube," is said to have "one cubic unit" of volume, and can be used to measure volume.	Major	24
5.MD.C.3b A solid figure which can be packed without gaps or overlaps using *n* unit cubes is said to have a volume of *n* cubic units.	Major	24
5.MD.C.4 Measure volumes by counting unit cubes, using cubic cm, cubic in, cubic ft, and improvised units.	Major	25
5.MD.C.5 Relate volume to the operations of multiplication and addition and solve real world and mathematical problems involving volume.	Major	26, 27
5.MD.C.5a Find the volume of a right rectangular prism with whole-number side lengths by packing it with unit cubes, and show that the volume is the same as would be found by multiplying the edge lengths, equivalently by multiplying the height by the area of the base. Represent threefold whole-number products as volumes, e.g., to represent the associative property of multiplication.	Major	26
5.MD.C.5b Apply the formulas $V = l \times w \times h$ and $V = b \times h$ for rectangular prisms to find volumes of right rectangular prisms with whole-number edge lengths in the context of solving real world and mathematical problems.	Major	26
5.MD.C.5c Recognize volume as additive. Find volumes of solid figures composed of two non-overlapping right rectangular prisms by adding the volumes of the non-overlapping parts, applying this technique to solve real world problems.	Major	27

The Standards for Mathematical Practice are integrated throughout the instructional lessons.

Common Core State Standards for Grade 5 Mathematics — Standards for Mathematical Content	Content Emphasis	Ready® Common Core Instruction Lesson(s)
Geometry		
Graph points on the coordinate plane to solve real-world and mathematical problems.		
5.G.A.1 Use a pair of perpendicular number lines, called axes, to define a coordinate system, with the intersection of the lines (the origin) arranged to coincide with the 0 on each line and a given point in the plane located by using an ordered pair of numbers, called its coordinates. Understand that the first number indicates how far to travel from the origin in the direction of one axis, and the second number indicates how far to travel in the direction of the second axis, with the convention that the names of the two axes and the coordinates correspond (e.g., x-axis and x-coordinate, y-axis and y-coordinate).	Supporting/ Additional	28
5.G.A.2 Represent real world and mathematical problems by graphing points in the first quadrant of the coordinate plane, and interpret coordinate values of points in the context of the situation.	Supporting/ Additional	29
Classify two-dimensional figures into categories based on their properties.		
5.G.B.3 Understand that attributes belonging to a category of two-dimensional figures also belong to all subcategories of that category. For example, all rectangles have four right angles and squares are rectangles, so all squares have four right angles.	Supporting/ Additional	31
5.G.B.4 Classify two-dimensional figures in a hierarchy based on properties.	Supporting/ Additional	30

The Standards for Mathematical Practice are integrated throughout the instructional lessons.